Betty an I
May.
be your.

Carroll E Hamilton

ALL SPIRITUAL BLESSINGS

THE BELIEVER'S SPIRITUAL WEALTH IN CHRIST

Carroll E. Hamilton

ALL SPIRITUAL BLESSINGS
The Believer's Spiritual Wealth in Christ

CARROLL E. HAMILTON
629 Yorktown Blvd
Locust Grove, VA 22508
PHONE: (540) 972-3051

E-MAIL: carroll-marian@juno.com
TO ORDER, CALL TOLL-FREE: 1-866-909-2665
ORDER ONLINE: http://www.xulonpress.com/bookstore

This Book Is Dedicated To
JESUS CHRIST
Who Enables Us To Experience
ALL SPIRITUAL BLESSINGS

CONTENTS

INTRODUCTION

Concerning his attempts to relate to everyone he met and to share the message of Christ, the Apostle Paul declared, "I do all this for the sake of the gospel, that I may share in its blessings" (1 Cor. 9:23). A blessing is a special benefit or favor. The Gospel provides many "blessings." The blessings of the Gospel are primarily spiritual blessings. My main purpose in writing this book is to show the variety of spiritual blessings that compose the Christian's spiritual wealth, how those blessing are appropriated and what they mean for this life and for eternity.

The number and variety of God's blessings are so great that an exhaustive study of them cannot be done in a single volume. I have tried to deal with topics that would give a comprehensive overview of spiritual blessings.

This book is sent out with a prayer that it will assist each reader to a greater understanding of the blessings of God and to a deeper experience of those blessings.

Carroll Hamilton
Locust Grove, Virginia

CHAPTER 1

ALL SPIRITUAL BLESSINGS

"Blessed be the God and Father of our Lord Jesus Christ, who has blessed us with all spiritual blessings in heavenly places in Christ" (Eph. 1:3 KJV).

Spiritual blessings may be contrasted with temporal or physical blessings. All persons enjoy God's temporal blessings. In His sermon on the mount Jesus said that God "...causes his sun to rise on the evil and the good, and sends rain on the righteous and the unrighteous" (Matt. 5:45b). However, spiritual blessings belong only to believers and those who are in the process of becoming believers. For believers there can be a spiritual aspect even to temporal blessings. In this book we will confine our study to those blessings that are primarily spiritual in nature. The Bible refers to "spiritual things," "spiritual understanding," "spiritual songs" and "spiritual wickedness," and has several references to "spiritual gifts," but the Scripture verse that opens this chapter is the only Bible reference to spiritual blessings. Yet they are implicit in almost every sentence of the New Testament.

PRAISE FOR SPIRITUAL BLESSINGS

The text above begins with Paul's praise to God for His many spiritual blessings. As God blesses us we can bless God by giving Him the praise He deserves. We do not deserve God's blessings, yet He has chosen to bless us and does so more abundantly than we can appreciate until He gives us "spiritual understanding" (Col. 1:9).

As Paul praises God he identifies Him as "the God and Father of our Lord Jesus Christ." The true and living God has made Himself known through His Son. The believer knows him as 'Jesus'—the One who Saves, as 'Christ'—the Anointed One of God, the Messiah promised in the Old Testament, and as 'Lord'—the One who deserves our worship, allegiance and obedience.

THE PROVIDER OF SPIRITUAL BLESSINGS

The Apostle Paul's praise was to God, "who has blessed us"— the One who is the provider of spiritual blessings. "Grace and peace to you from God our Father and the Lord Jesus Christ" (Eph. 1:2).

God provides His blessings by grace, apart from anything we can do to earn or deserve them. My testimony to God's grace can best be given in the words of John Newton:

> "Amazing grace! how sweet the sound, That
>   saved a wretch like me!
> I once was lost, but now am found, Was
>   blind, but now I see.
>
> 'Twas grace that taught my heart to fear, And
>   grace my fears relieved;
> How precious did that grace appear The hour
>   I first believed!"

God provides His blessings as 'our Father.' His love prompts Him to bless His children in every way possible. He blesses us by what He gives and by what He withholds. Jesus assured us, "...your Father knows what you need before you ask him" (Matt. 6:8). "Every good and perfect gift is from above, coming down from the Father of the heavenly lights" (James 1:17).

God provides 'all spiritual blessings' through "the Lord Jesus Christ." "I... thank God for...his grace given you in Christ Jesus" (I Cor. 1:4). All of God's blessings are made possible through the "...one mediator between God and men, the man Christ Jesus" (I Tim. 2:5).

THE PARTICIPANTS IN SPIRITUAL BLESSINGS

My text says that God has blessed "us." In this case the 'us' referred to the believers who received Paul's letter. We may interpret the 'us' to be all believers living today. Everyone who has come to know God through Jesus Christ participates in the benefits of 'all spiritual blessings.'

God desires that everyone be recipients of His spiritual blessings. "God our Savior,...wants all men to be saved and to come to a knowledge of the truth" (1 Tim. 2:3b, 4). Peter wrote that the Lord Jesus delays His return to earth, "...not wanting anyone to perish, but everyone to come to repentance" (II Peter 3:9b).

God has made it possible for everyone who is willing to receive His blessings. "For God so loved the world, that he gave his only begotten Son, that whosoever believeth in him should not perish, but have everlasting life" (John 3:16 KJV). God makes His blessings available because of His love for all persons in the world. He loves you and me! We become recipients of all spiritual blessings when we believe "in him," depending on Jesus who paid our sin debt on the cross, as our way to escape from perishing. We receive "everlasting life" by receiving Him into our lives as Lord and Savior.

THE PLENTITUDE OF SPIRITUAL BLESSINGS

The believer can benefit from "all spiritual blessings." In spite of the title of this book, I will hardly discuss them all. They are almost like "...the sand of the seashore, which cannot...be counted" (Hosea 1:10).

Notice the list of spiritual blessings to be found just in the first chapter of Ephesians, verses 4-14: God "chose us in him [Christ]; "chose us...to be holy and blameless in his sight;" "predestined us to be adopted as his sons;" "his glorious grace ...he has given us in the One he loves;" "In him we have redemption..., the forgiveness of sins;" "God's grace...lavished on us;" "with all wisdom and understanding ...he made known to us the mystery of his will;" "his good pleasure ...to bring all things in heaven and on earth together under one head, even Christ;" "that we...in Christ...might be for the praise of his glory;" "included in Christ when you heard...the gospel of your salvation;" "marked with a seal, the promised Holy Spirit;" "the...Holy Spirit...is a deposit guaranteeing our inheritance;" that guarantee is "...until the redemption of those who are God's possession."

These incomparable blessings should give every believer some holy hallelujahs!

THE PRODUCER OF SPIRITUAL BLESSINGS

While God the Father provides spiritual blessings,

their very name tells us they are produced by the Holy
Spirit. They are 'spiritual blessings,' pertaining to the
Spirit. In the section above we read about believers
being sealed by the Spirit and receiving the Holy
Spirit as a 'deposit.' The Holy Spirit in the believer's
life is God's mark of ownership, the seal of authenticity. The Holy Spirit is also God's 'earnest money' that
He has put up as a guarantee that what He has begun
in the believer's life will be carried on to completion
when Jesus returns in glory.

THE PLACE OF SPIRITUAL BLESSINGS

The believer is blessed "in heavenly places." A
literal reading from the original language would
simply be 'in the heavenlies.' The only use of this
expression in the Bible is in the Letter to the
Ephesians where it occurs five times. The second
occurrence says, "That power is like the working of
his mighty strength, which he exerted in Christ when
he raised him from the dead and seated him at his
right hand in the heavenly realms" (Eph. 1:19b, 20).
Here 'the heavenlies' describes the place where
Jesus is seated at the right hand of God the Father.

The next occurrence sheds more light on the
meaning of the term. "And God raised us up with
Christ and seated us with him in the heavenly realms
in Christ Jesus" (Eph. 2:6). In Paul's Letter to the
Romans he wrote, "Now if we died with Christ, we
believe that we will also live with him" (6:8). Here
he is talking about the believer's identification with
Jesus in His death, burial and resurrection. One who

is "in Christ" is living a new life "with Him." In Him we are already seated 'in the heavenlies,' the place of victory, rest, honor and authority.

The other two references to the heavenlies are: "His intent was that now, through the church, the manifold wisdom of God should be made known to the rulers and authorities in the heavenly realms" (Eph. 3:10); "For our struggle is not against flesh and blood, but against the rulers, against the authorities, against the powers of this dark world and against the spiritual forces of evil in the heavenly realms" (Eph. 6:12). These references show that the heavenlies include the area where the unseen spiritual forces of the universe are at work, even Satan and his demons. Through the Church God is demonstrating His victory over the forces of evil. Is His victory being demonstrated in your life and the life of your church?

THE PROCURING OF SPIRITUAL BLESSINGS

Spiritual blessings belong to those who are "in Christ." I have already said that we get into Christ by receiving Him into our lives as Lord and Savior. There will be more about that in the next three chapters.

Once we are 'in Christ' it is possible for us to not fully possess our possessions. I read about an English nobleman who died and left a rather sizeable estate. He had no direct descendants, but according to British law his estate would pass to his nearest relative. A search was made, and that heir was finally located in the United States. When the man received word of his good fortune, he went to the nearest town, bought a new suit of clothes and began making preparation to sail to England. A reporter asked the man, "Where are you going?" He replied, "To take possession of my estate."

The believer's "estate" includes 'all spiritual blessings.' It is a large estate of considerable wealth. Our Benefactor died and rose again. His will has been through probate and He is the executor of His own estate. He is dispensing it to each believer according to our need. Yet it is possible for believers to frustrate what the Lord wishes to do in and through our lives. I once knew a lady who owned property worth several hundred thousand dollars. But she lived in a small house that needed painting and had no indoor plumbing other than at the kitchen sink. She had resources she could have used, but by her own choice she lived almost like a pauper. I wonder how many Christians there are who live like spiritual paupers.

Once after I preached on the Scripture verse that I am using as the text for this chapter, a lady in the congregation said, "I have always thought of spiritual blessings as being automatic for Christians." As faith begins our Christian walk, so we continue to experience our Lord's blessings by faith. "For we walk by faith, not by sight" (II Cor. 5:7, KJV). The Bible defines faith when it says, "Now faith is the substance of things hoped for, the evidence of things not seen" (Heb. 11:1 KJV). The believer has no doubt that spiritual blessings are real even though in most cases they cannot be seen by the physical eye. Faith gives substance to the hope that we know to be real by the evidence which God supplies to our heart when we believe and act on His Word. This is not to imply that genuine faith is merely subjective, for faith rests on the objective Words of God in the Bible.

Unfortunately, some who read this book will add themselves to the group described in the following Scripture verse: "...the message they heard was of no value to them, because those who heard did not combine it with faith" (Heb. 4:2b). The object of the believer's faith is God as He reveals Himself in the Bible. That revelation is the subject of the next chapter. The reward of the believer's faith is to experience "all spiritual blessings."

CHAPTER 2

REVELATION

*The secret things belong to the Lord our
God, but the things revealed belong to us.
Deut. 29:29a*

Revelation is not the greatest of God's blessings,
but is of first importance. By "revelation" I
mean the efforts and ability of God to communicate
with persons living in this world. Without revelation
we could have no knowledge of other spiritual
blessings.

THE COMMUNICATION OF GOD'S
REVELATION

Our Creator is capable of communicating with
his creatures. Revelation uproots the idea that if
there is a God He cannot be known.

Revelation is conveyed even in *the skies*. "The

heavens declare the glory of God; the skies proclaim the works of his hands" (Psa. 19:1). This reflection of God's glory in His creation is a universal revelation. "Their voice goes out into all the earth, their words to the ends of the world" (Psa. 19:4). In creation we behold the handiwork of our Creator. "What may be known about God is plain to them, because God has made it plain to them. For since the creation of the world God's invisible qualities—his eternal power and divine nature—have been clearly seen, being understood from what has been made, so that men are without excuse" (Rom. 1:19, 20). Creation argues convincingly that there is a divine Creator who is infinite in power.

But God communicates with us even more clearly and completely in *the Scriptures*. The Bible is a dependable revelation from God. Jesus assured us, "...the Scriptures cannot be broken" (John 10:35). The psalmist prayed, "All your words are true" (Psa. 119:160). Paul taught that God inspired the human authors of the Bible so that what they wrote is a faithful revelation from Him. "All Scripture is God-breathed and useful for teaching, rebuking, correcting and training in righteousness" (II Tim. 3:16). The Bible reveals all that we need to know about God and our relationship to Him.

This written Word of God tells us about His supreme revelation in Jesus, the living Word of God. God speaks through Scripture, but He speaks most eloquently through Jesus Christ, *the Son of God*. "In the past God spoke to our forefathers through the prophets at many times and in various ways, but in these last days he has spoken to us by his Son, whom he appointed heir of all things, and through whom he made the universe. The Son is the radiance of God's glory and the exact representation of his being, sustaining all things by his powerful word" (Heb. 1:1-3). How blessed we are that Jesus lived on earth as "the exact representation" of God. He came as the visible manifestation of the invisible God. "No one has even seen God, but God the One and Only, who is at the Father's side, has made him known" (John 1:18).

Jesus is the only sufficient revelation of God, for Jesus declared, "All things have been committed to me by my Father. No one knows the Son except the Father, and no one knows the Father except the Son and those to whom the Son chooses to reveal him" (Matt. 11:27). Jesus taught that He was sent by God: "...I am not here on my own, but he who sent me is true. You do not know him, but I know him because I am from him and he sent me" (John 7:28, 29). Jesus also taught that to know Him is to know God. "'You do not know me or my Father' Jesus replied. 'If you knew me, you would know my father also'" (John 8:19). Jesus told his disciples, "Anyone who has seen me has seen the Father" (John 8:19). In Gethsemane Jesus prayed, "I have revealed you to those whom you gave me out of the world" (John 17:6).

To be a person whom God has given to Jesus you must believe in Him as God's ultimate revelation to you, for Jesus taught, "When a man believes in me, he does not believe in me only, but in the one who sent me. When he looks to me, he sees the one who sent me. I have come into the world as a light, so that no one who believes in me should stay in darkness" (John 12:44-46).

We are blessed that God takes the initiative in making Himself known to us through Jesus. "For God who said, 'Let light shine out of darkness,' made his light shine in our hearts to give us the light of the knowledge of the glory of God in the face of Christ" (II Cor. 4:6). The light of God's revelation dispels spiritual darkness for all who are open to the truth of *Scripture* concerning the *Son of God.*

All true spiritual revelation involves *the Spirit of God.* Only with the aid of the Holy Spirit do we recognize the revelation of God in the skies. The Scriptures are revelation because, "...no prophecy of Scripture came about by the prophet's own interpretation. For prophecy never had its origin in the will of man, but men spoke from God as they were carried along by the Holy Spirit" (II Peter 1:20, 21). That Jesus is the unique Son of God can be fully known only when that revelation is made understandable by the Holy Spirit. Jesus explained, "But when he, the Spirit of truth, comes, he will guide you into all truth. He will not speak on his own; he will speak only what he hears, and he will tell you what is yet to come. He will bring glory to me by taking from what is mine and making it known to you" (John 16:13, 14). More attention to the Spirit's role in revelation will be given later in this chapter.

THE CONTENT OF GOD'S REVELATION

The message of revelation is as broad as all the subjects of the Bible. However, a few themes stand like majestic mountain peaks on the landscape of Scripture. First and foremost God's revelation is *Self-revelation.* As He reveals Himself, God is saying, "I want you to know Me!"

Here I will give only a brief summary of some of the main attributes of God. The Bible begins by revealing God as Creator. "In the beginning God created the heavens and the earth" (Gen. 1:1). He reveals Himself as the only true God and as One who is worthy of worship. "But the Lord is the true God; he is the living God, the eternal King" (Jer. 10:10). "All nations will come and worship before you, for your righteous acts have been revealed" (Rev. 15:4).

God's most important attribute may be summed up in the title Loving Father. "Praise be to the God and Father of our Lord Jesus Christ, the Father of compassion and the God of all comfort" (II Cor. 1:3). "God is love" (I John 4:8).

God is omnipotent (all powerful). "Jesus looked at them and said, 'With man this is impossible, but not with God; all things are possible with God" (Mark 10:27). God is omniscient (all knowing). "The eyes of the Lord are everywhere, keeping watch on the wicked and the good" (Prov. 15:3). Jesus said concerning God's knowledge of us, "Indeed the very hairs of your head are all numbered" (Luke 12:7). God is omnipresent (present everywhere). "'Do not I fill heaven and earth?' declares the Lord" (Jer. 23:24).

God is merciful and gracious. "He is kind to the ungrateful and wicked" (Luke 6:35). God is holy and just. "But just as he who called you is holy, so be holy in all you do; for it is written, 'Be holy, because I am holy" (I Peter 1:15). "good and upright is the Lord" (Psa. 25:8). Because of His justice God is an impartial judge. "For God does not show favoritism" (Rom. 2:11). "This will take place on the day when God will judge men's secrets through Jesus Christ" (Rom. 2:16).

The tallest peak on the landscape of Scripture has many names all summed up in the title *Savior.* Before the birth of Jesus to the virgin Mary, an angel of the Lord had said, "Joseph son of David, do not be afraid to take Mary home as your wife, because what is conceived in her is from the Holy Spirit. She will give birth to a son, and you are to give him the name Jesus, because he will save his people from their sins" (Matt. 1:20, 21).

The message of the angel to the Judean shepherds is not just for the Christmas season. This "...good news of great joy...for all the people," tells us "...a Savor has been born to you; he is Christ the Lord" (Luke 2:10-11). As the public ministry of Jesus was about to begin some thirty years later, John the Baptist announced, "Look, the Lamb of God, who takes away the sin of the world!" (John 1:29).

After the Samaritans of the village of Sychar heard Jesus preach some of them said, "Now we have heard for ourselves, and we know that this man really is the Savior of the world" (John 4:42). On another occasion Jesus said concerning himself, "For the Son of Man came to seek and to save what was lost" (Luke 19:10).

Jesus became the Savior of the world by dying for our sins on the cross. After His resurrection and ascension back to heaven, Peter referred to Jesus as he preached, "Salvation is found in no one else, for there is no other name under heaven given to men by which we must be saved" (Acts 4:12). A more detailed look at the Saviorhood of Jesus will be found in the chapter entitled "Redeemer."

Next to Mount Savior is a beautiful peak called *Salvation.* In the New Testament salvation usually refers to spiritual deliverance from the penalty and power of sin. It will ultimately mean deliverance from the presence of sin following physical death. Many synonyms and theological terms are used in an effort to explain the full meaning of salvation. It is adoption, eternal life, forgiveness, freedom, reconciliation, regeneration and numerous other concepts that are necessary to fully express all that God does for the person who receives the salvation provided by the Savior. What God has revealed about salvation will be more fully explored in the chapters on Redemption.

Salvation is necessary because of the presence of Mount *Sin* which at first appears attractive, but a closer look shows that it is ugly, even hideous. The prevalence of sin is complete. "For all have sinned and fall short of the glory of God" (Rom. 3:23). The power of sin is great. "Everyone who sins is a slave to sin" (John 8:34). The penalty of sin is sure. "The wages of sin is death" (Rom. 6:23). "Sin when it is full-grown, gives birth to death" (James 1:15).

The death caused by sin is spiritual as well as physical. It separates the sinner from God. But note the last of Rom. 6:23, "...the gift of God is eternal life in Christ Jesus our Lord." Our Creator could not bear to have His creatures perish in sin if He could provide a way of salvation. The ability of God was demonstrated in His provision of a Savior. God's remedy for sin was provided through the sacrifice of His Son. These are the great themes of Scripture that we will seek to amplify in the following pages. Hopefully, this amplification will give us a fuller appreciation for "all spiritual blessings."

THE COMPREHENSION OF GOD'S REVELATION

Even though God has clearly revealed Himself persons are inclined to reject His revelation. "The man without the Spirit does not accept the things that come from the Spirit of God for they are fool-ishness to him, and he cannot understand them because they are spiritually discerned" (I Cor. 2:14). This lack of capacity to understand spiritual truth is due to the fact that outside of Christ, persons are spiritually dead. God created us as triune beings with body, soul and spirit. When Adam and Eve sinned they died spiritually. As their descendents we are born as persons alive in body and soul but dead in spirit. Being born spiritually into the kingdom of

God restores our spiritual discernment and capacity to worship God "in spirit and truth" (John 4:23).

People turn away from God's revelation because "...men loved darkness instead of light because their deeds were evil" (John 3:19). Their rejection of God's revelation is encouraged by the deception from Satan. "The god of this age has blinded the minds of unbelievers so that they cannot see the light of the gospel of the glory of Christ who is the image of God" (II Cor. 4:4). This does not mean that persons can excuse their rejection of truth by saying, "The devil made me do it!"

The light of revelation still reaches us because God takes the initiative in making Himself known. Romans 10:20 quotes from the words of God through the prophet Isaiah, "I was found by those who did not seek me; I revealed myself to those who did not ask for me."

As God reaches out to us the amount of revelation we receive depends on our response. Comprehending spiritual truth requires *an open mind.* Jesus prayed, "I praise you, Father, Lord of heaven and earth, because you have hidden these things from the wise and learned, and revealed them to little children" (Matt. 11:25). A child-like spirit implies not only an open mind, but also *a willingness to be taught.* Jesus invites us, "Take my yoke upon you and learn from me" (Matt. 11:29).

Receiving God's revelation also requires *a willingness to obey* what we learn. This is seen in the following words of Jesus, "If anyone chooses to do God's will, he will find out whether my teaching comes from God or whether I speak on my own" (John 9:17). How blessed we are to have this promise concerning a search to know God's will. This is a promise that may be claimed by every honest doubter.

We comprehend God's revelation only when we are *committed to following the path of truth* wherever it may lead. Forget not the words of Jesus as He stood before Pilate, "Everyone on the side of truth listens to me" (John 19:37).

The comprehension of spiritual truth requires *the leadership of the Spirit of God.* His leadership is available to the born again believer. "We have not received the spirit of the world but the Spirit who is from God, that we may understand what God has freely given us" (I Cor. 2:12). Illumination is the theological term for this work of the Spirit.

The Holy Spirit enables the unbeliever to become aware of God's revelation and to become a believer by receiving the truth of God. Jesus said concerning the Holy Spirit, "He will convict the world of guilt in regard to sin and righteousness and judgment" (John 16:8). This ministry of the Spirit is involved where Jesus said, "No one can come to me unless the Father who sent me draws him" (John 6:44). As the Father draws through the Spirit, the person under conviction becomes *aware of his need* of forgiveness of sin and of his opportunity to receive it through Jesus Christ. "Yet to all who received him [Jesus], to those who believed in his name, he gave the right to become Children of God" (John 1:12).

THE CONSEQUENCES OF GOD'S REVELATION

The response of persons to God's revelation divides the world into two camps. Jesus asked, "Do you think I came to bring peace on earth?" Then He answered His question, "No, I tell you but division" (Luke 12:51). Acceptance or rejection of God's revelation in Jesus determines whether a person is saved or lost, believer or unbeliever, righteous or unrighteous.

Revelation is available to everyone. John wrote concerning the beginning of the ministry of Jesus, "The true light that gives light to every man was coming into the world" (John 1:9). An earlier verse said, "...through him all men might believe" (John 1:7).

Those who reject God's revelation remain separated from God in sin. They are doomed to experience deepening spiritual darkness as long as they turn from the light of God. "For although they knew God, they neither glorified him as God nor gave thanks to him, but their thinking became futile and their foolish hearts were darkened (Rom. 1:21)

The reception of revealed truth has many beneficial consequences. God's revelation *discloses truth* as we see in the words of Jesus: "'If you hold to my teaching, you really are my disciples. Then you will know the truth, and the truth will set you free'" (John 8:31b, 32). Jesus Himself is Ultimate Truth for He declared, "I am the way and the truth and the life. No one comes to the Father except through me"

(John 14:6). "Stand firm then, with the belt of truth buckled around your waist" (Eph. 6:14).

Receiving God's revelation *imparts knowledge.* The greatest knowledge is to know God. Jesus prayed, "Now this is eternal life: that they may know you, the only true God, and Jesus Christ whom you have sent" (John 17:3). We may know God through His Son. Paul wrote, "My purpose is...that they may know the mystery of God, namely, Christ, in whom are hidden all the treasures of wisdom and knowledge" (Col. 2:2, 3).

Receiving God's revelation also *provides light.* Matthew tells us that by living in Capernaum during one phase of His public ministry, Jesus fulfilled the prophecy of Isaiah 9:2, "The people walking in darkness have seen a great light; on those living in the land of the shadow of death a light has dawned" (quoted in Matt. 4:16). Those who do not know God personally are "walking in darkness" whether they realize it or not. "The light shines in the darkness but the darkness has not understood it" (John 1:5). Jesus declared, "I am the light of the world. Whoever follows me will never walk in darkness, but will have the light of life" (John 8:12). Jesus warned, "Put your trust in the light while you have it, so that you may become sons of light" (John 12:36).

There is an *experience of* great *joy* for the person who responds to revelation by receiving the salvation God has provided. "With joy you will draw water from the wells of salvation" (Isa.12:3). The believer may experience the joy of which Jesus spoke when He said, "I have told you this so that my joy may be in you and that your joy may be complete" (John 15:11).

Receiving God's revelation also *gives* the *peace* mentioned in Romans 5:1, "Therefore, since we have been justified through faith, we have peace with God through our Lord Jesus Christ." Jesus promised peace to His followers with these words, "Peace I leave with you; my peace I give to you. I do not give to you as the world gives. Do not let your hearts be troubled and not be afraid" (John 14:27).

Revelation *produces* an eternal *hope* in the lives of all who respond by receiving Jesus as their Savior and Lord. "Praise be to the God and Father of our Lord Jesus Christ! In his great mercy he has given us new birth into a living hope through the resurrection of Jesus Christ! (I Peter 1:3). Dear reader, my prayer for you is one of Paul's prayers for the Romans: "May the God of hope fill you with all joy and peace as you trust in him, so that you may overflow with hope by the power of the Holy Spirit" (Rom. 15:13).

CHAPTER 3

REDEEMER

When Christ came as high priest...He did not enter by means of the blood of goats and calves; but he entered the Most Holy Place once and for all by his own blood, having obtained eternal redemption. Hebrews 9:11a, 12

Some people subscribe to a humanistic philosophy that would strip Christian theology of all elements of the supernatural. They think of Jesus as a fellow human being who is unique only in that He has given the world a worthy example of how a person should relate to society and to other persons. Such a belief is completely foreign to the faith of New Testament Christians.

The New Testament presents Jesus as infinitely more than a good example to follow. He is the One Person of all history through whom persons may become properly related to God. Only Jesus can remove the guilt of sin separating us from God. Only through Jesus can one who is dead in sin be transformed into a saint of God. The message of the Scripture cited above is that Jesus became the Redeemer by His sacrifice on the cross. Jesus is the only One who can meet the deepest needs of the human heart and remedy the most serious deficiencies of human nature. Jesus is the Redeemer provided by God in wisdom and love.

My message to you is that the redeeming Christ has power to change human nature and remedy all the effects of sin because of who He is, what He has done, what He is doing and what He shall do. All spiritual blessings are ours through our perfect Redeemer.

Jesus is qualified to redeem all who come to God through Him because of

WHO HE IS

Jesus is the unique God-Man, the Third Person of the triune God-Head. The deity of Jesus is seen in *His vital pre-existence*. Micah 5:2 identified the promised Redeemer as One whose "...goings forth are from long ago, From the days of eternity" (NAS). During His public ministry Jesus declared, "Before Abraham was, I am" (John 6:58).

Jesus is the eternal Son of God existing with the Father in all of past eternity. This is one of the reasons He is qualified to be the Redeemer. "Who [Jesus] being the brightness of his [God's] glory, and the express image of his person, and upholding all things by the word of his power, when he had by himself purged our sins, sat down on the right hand of the Majesty on high" (Heb. 1:3).

Belief in the deity of Jesus is a condition of receiving the redemption He provides. "Whosoever shall confess that Jesus is the Son of God, God dwelleth in him and he in God" (I John 4:15 KJV). Jesus warned, "If you do not believe that I am the one I claim to be you will indeed die in your sins" (John 8:24).

Before Roman Emperor Theodosius became known as a Christian, it is reported that he denied the deity of Jesus. Bishop Amphilocus was present when Theodosius was giving his son Arcadius a ruling position in the empire. At the occasion Bishop Amphilocus gave an address without making any mention of Arcadius.

Theodosius asked, "What! Do you take no notice of my son?"

Amphilocus replied, "Sire, you do so highly resent my apparent neglect of your son, because I do not give him equal honors with yourself. Then what must the eternal God think of you when you degrade His co-equal and co-eternal Son to the level of His creatures?"

Jesus was referring to God the Father when He promised, "He who receives me receives the one who sent me" (Matt. 10:40).

Jesus is also qualified to be our redeemer because of His humanity, because He is man as well as God. The eternal Son of God became the Son of Man by

His virgin birth. "All this took place to fulfill what the Lord had said through the prophet: 'The virgin will be with child and will give birth to a son, and they will call him Immanuel—which means, 'God with us'" (Matt. 1:22, 23). Because God holds persons accountable for their sins, Jesus had to become human to become our Sin Bearer and Redeemer.

Jesus is also qualified to be the world's Redeemer because of

WHAT HE HAS DONE

It was by *His voluntary incarnation* that Jesus entered this world. "Who, being in very nature God, did not consider equality with God something to be grasped, but made himself nothing, taking the very nature of a servant, being made in human likeness" (Phil. 2:6, 7).

In the previous chapter we saw that by His incarnation Jesus revealed God to this world. By becoming like His creatures, Jesus was able to show us our need and to meet that need. "For what the law was powerless to do in that it was weakened by the sinful nature, God did by sending his own Son in the likeness of sinful man to be a sin offering. And so he condemned sin in sinful man" (Rom. 8:3).

Because of *His virtuous life* Jesus could become our Redeemer. Since He committed no sin during His earthly life, Jesus could die as our sin-bearer. The Bible calls Jesus, "...a lamb without blemish of defect" (I Peter 1:19), and assures us, "...in him is no sin" (I John 3:5).

Because of the righteous life of Jesus we may become righteous. "God made him who had no sin to be sin for us, so that in him we might become the righteousness of God" (I Cor. 5:21). Later a whole chapter will be devoted to the blessing of righteousness.

The virtuous life of Jesus is valuable to us because it was concluded by *His vicarious death*. "For what I received I passed on to you as of first importance: that Christ died for our sins according to the Scriptures" (I Cor. 15:3). Our need and the provision of Jesus is expressed in these words: "Christ redeemed us from the curse of the law, by becoming a curse for us" (Gal. 3:13). The curse belonging to you and me for breaking the moral law of God was borne by Jesus as He died on the cross.

As a raging forest fire approached his property a man responded by setting another fire. He explained his action by saying, "The fire cannot come where the fire has already been." The fire of judgment against your sin and mine has fallen on Jesus on the cross. When we place our faith in the sacrificial death of Jesus we are in the place of safety and redemption, for "the fire cannot come where the fire has already been."

Jesus is the Redeemer because His death was followed by *His vindicative resurrection*. "He was raised on the third day according to the Scriptures" (I Cor. 15:4). The New Testament carefully links the death and resurrection of Jesus as inseparable events. "He was delivered over to death for our sins and was raised to life for our justification" (Rom.

4:25). The blessing of being justified in the sight of God is ours when we depend on the finished work of our Redeemer as the sure basis of our being redeemed from the guilt of sin.

The resurrection of Jesus authenticated and vindicated all that He taught and all that He claimed concerning Himself. He is indeed the divine Son of God with power to save all who come to God through Him.

Forty days after His resurrection, the disciples of Jesus witnessed *His visible ascension.* "He was taken up before their very eyes, and a cloud hid him from their sight" (Acts 1:9). The Apostle Paul explained the meaning of the ascension with these words, "Therefore God exalted him to the highest place and gave him the name that is above every name, that at the name of Jesus every knee should bow, in heaven and on earth and under the earth, and every tongue confess that Jesus Christ is Lord, to the glory of God the Father" (Phil. 2:9-11).

The Redeemer is exalted as Lord over all God's creation and over all created beings. His is the supreme name in all the universe. Jesus said, "All authority in heaven and on earth has been given to me" (Matt. 28:18). What Jesus has done qualifies Him as Redeemer.

WHAT HE IS DOING

The Present ministry of Jesus is in behalf of those who have trusted him as their Redeemer from the penalty and power of sin: *His valid intercession.*

"Christ Jesus...is at the right hand of God and is also interceding for us" (Rom. 8:34). This is a unique ministry belonging only to Jesus. "For there is one God and one mediator between God and men, the man Christ Jesus" (I Tim. 2:5).

Jesus is personally administering the redemption He has provided for those who receive Him into their lives. "For this reason Christ is the mediator of a new covenant, that those who are called may receive the promised eternal inheritance" (Heb. 9:15).

Jesus is the believer's defense attorney pleading our case before the Father. "My little children, I write this to you so that you will not sin. But if anyone does sin, we have one who speaks to the Father in our defense—Jesus Christ, the righteous One" (I John 2:1).

Another title associated with the Redeemer's intercession is High Priest. A priest represents man to God and God to man. "We do have such a high priest, who sat down at the right hand of the throne of the Majesty in heaven" (Heb. 8:1). Jesus is a sympathetic priest who knows our needs even better than we do. "For we do not have a high priest who is unable to sympathize with our weaknesses, but we have one who was tempted in every way, just as we are—yet was without sin. Let us then approach the throne of grace with confidence, so that we may receive mercy and find grace to help us in our time of need" (Heb. 4:15, 16).

The Redeemer's intercession is continuous and adequate for every believer. "Therefore he is able to save completely those who come to God through him, because he always lives to intercede for them" (Heb. 7:25).

WHAT HE SHALL DO

The climax of the ministry of Jesus shall be *His victorious return.* "Look, he is coming with the clouds, and every eye shall see him" (Rev. 1:7). The blessing of redemption will then be complete. Although the believer already possesses eternal life, his physical body is not yet redeemed: "...we ourselves, who have the firstfruits of the Spirit, groan inwardly as we wait eagerly for our adoption as sons, the redemption of our bodies" (Rom. 8:23). This "redemption" is the physical resurrection of our bodies at the second coming of Jesus. A later chapter is devoted to the blessing of resurrection.

The believer has been redeemed from the penalty and power of sin. When Jesus returns, believers shall be forever redeemed from the presence of sin: "...so Christ was sacrificed once to take away the sins of many people; and he will appear a second time, not to bear sin, but to bring salvation to those who are waiting for him" (Heb. 10:28). The redemptive work begun in the heart of the believer at the moment of his of her conversion will be completed when the Redeemer returns to this earth. "Dear friends, now are we children of God, and what we will be has not yet been made known. But we know that when he appears, we shall be like him, for we shall see him as he is" (I John 3:2).

Dear reader, if you have not received the

Redeemer as your own, please remember that:
"...Christ Jesus...has become for us...our...redemption" (I Cor. 1:30b). You receive redemption by
receiving the Redeemer. "Everyone who calls on the
name of the Lord will be saved" (Rom. 10:13). You
may call on Him with faith that He is able and
anxious to save all who depend on Him for salvation
from the penalty and power of sin.

CHAPTER 4

REDEMPTION (Part I)

"In love he predestined us to be adopted as his sons through Jesus Christ, in accordance with his pleasure and will—to the praise of his glorious grace, which he has freely given us in the One he loves. In him we have redemption through his blood, the forgiveness of sins, in accordance with the riches of God's grace" (Eph. 1:4b-7).

Webster's New World Dictionary defines redeem as "...to buy back;...to pay off (a mortgage or note);...to set free;...to deliver from sin and its penalties, as by a sacrifice made for the sinner; to...atone for."

In this chapter redemption will be used primarily as a synonym for salvation in all its ramifications. Because it answers our greatest need, redemption is the greatest of all spiritual blessings.

Redemption is based on two things: God's provision of redemption and an individual's response to God's offer of redemption. In the previous chapter we saw that Jesus is the Redeemer God has provided.

GOD'S PROVISION OF REDEMPTION

Only God possesses *the power to provide redemption.* "I am not ashamed of the gospel, because it is the power of God for the salvation of everyone who believes" (Rom. 1:16). Redemption concerns the Good News of God's saving power through Jesus Christ.

Even though we are totally undeserving of redemption it has been *provided by God's grace* (His unmerited favor toward us). "We believe it is through the grace of our Lord Jesus that we are saved" (Acts 15:11). We are totally dependent on God's grace because we are totally lacking in ability to save ourselves. "I do not set aside the grace of God, for if righteousness could be gained through the law, Christ died for nothing" (Gal. 2:21). "In him we have redemption...in accordance with the riches of God's grace" (Eph. 1:7). Paul also wrote to the Ephesian believers, "For it is by grace you have been saved" (Eph. 2:8).

Redemption has been *provided by God's calling and appointment.* "But we ought always to thank God for you, brothers loved by the Lord, because from the beginning God chose you to be saved through the sanctifying work of the Spirit and through belief in the truth" (II Thess. 2:13). God has chosen to save all who come to Him by way of the redemption He has provided. The believer is also said to be appointed to salvation: "For God did not appoint us to suffer wrath but to receive salvation through our Lord Jesus Christ" (I Thess. 5:9).

Believers are redeemed *through the saving message God has provided.* "For the message of the cross is foolishness to those who are perishing, but to us who are being saved it is the power of God" (I Cor. 1:18). This powerful message of the Cross is found in the Bible. Paul reminded Timothy, "...from infancy you have known the holy Scriptures, which are able to make you wise for salvation through faith in Christ Jesus" (II Tim. 3:15). This message was announced by the Lord and its authenticity was confirmed by His followers. (Heb. 2:3).

The saving message of the Cross is the Gospel or Good News of redemption through the death and resurrection of Jesus. "By this gospel you are saved, if you hold firmly to the word I preached to you" (I Cor. 15:2). The message of God's provision of redemption must be heard and understood before an individual can respond to it. "And you also were included in Christ when you heard the word of truth, the gospel of your salvation" (Eph. 1:13). "How, then, can they call on the one they have not believed in? And how can they believe in the one of whom they have not heard? (Rom. 10:14a).

Some people hear the Good News preached and reject it. However, it saves only those who believe it as revealed truth. "For since in the wisdom of God the world through its wisdom did not know him, God was pleased through the foolishness of what was preached to save those who believe" (I Cor. 1:21).

In the previous chapter we saw that redemption is *provided through Jesus* by virtue of who He is, what He has done, what He is doing and what He shall do. "For God did not send his Son into the world to condemn the world but to save the world" (John 3:17). Paul testified, "Therefore I endure everything for the sake of the elect, that they too may obtain the salvation that is in Christ Jesus" (II Tim. 2:10). Jesus is called "the author of salvation" (Heb. 3:10) and "the source of eternal salvation" (Heb. 5:9).

Redemption is also provided *through the work of the Holy Spirit* in the life of individuals who have not experienced salvation. When the Gospel is heard the Spirit of God enlightens the sinner to his or her need of the redemption made available through the Redeemer. The Holy Spirit brings to the sinner the sense of guilt that David felt when he confessed to God, "Against you, you only, have I sinned and done what is evil in your sight" (Psa. 51:4).

The Holy Spirit convinces the sinner that Jesus is God's sufficient provision for redemption. He makes real the claim of Jesus when He declared, "But I, when I am lifted up from the earth, will draw all men to myself" (John 12:32).

God has provided redemption as *a free gift*. "For it is by grace you have been saved, through faith—and this not from yourselves, it is the gift of God—not by works, so that no one can boast" (Eph. 2:8, 9). Salvation is received, not as a reward, but as an inheritance. "Are not all angels ministering spirits sent to serve those who will inherit salvation?" (Heb. 1:14).

A PERSON'S RESPONSE TO THE OFFER OF REDEMPTION

Whether or not a person receives the redemption God has provided depends entirely on his response to a personal encounter with the living Christ. A positive response of receiving Christ depends on *a person's willingness to come to God* on His terms. The Bible says concerning Jesus, "He came to that which was his own, but his own did not receive him" (John 1:12). The response of Jesus to this rejection is seen in His lament, "O Jerusalem, Jerusalem, you who kill the prophets and stone those sent to you, how often I have longed to gather your children together, as a hen gathers her chicks under her wings, but you were not willing" (Matt. 23:37). Jesus longs to have a personal relationship with you and me. He desires that everyone know Him as Savior and Lord.

Before a person will come to God on His terms there must be *a recognition of need.* To the Pharisees who took pride in their morality and detailed efforts to fulfill the law, Jesus said, "I tell you the truth, the tax collectors and prostitutes are entering the kingdom of God ahead of you" (Matt. 21:31). No person is so righteous that he does not need redemption. Jesus declared, "It is not the healthy who need a doctor, but the sick. I have not come to call the righteous but sinners" (Mark 2:17).

We are not sinners because we sin; we sin because we are sinners. The essence of sin is that we have decided to be our own lord rather that letting God have His rightful place in our lives. Without exception this is a problem of every person in the world. "But the Scripture declares that the whole world is a prisoner of sin" (Gal. 3:22).

When a person recognizes the fact of his sin and need for the redemption Jesus has provided, the first condition of salvation is *repentance.* Repentance includes a person's sorrow for his rebellion against God and a willingness, with God's help, to turn from sin to receive Jesus as Savior and Lord. "Godly sorrow brings repentance that leads to salvation and leaves no regret, but worldly sorrow brings death" (II Cor. 7:10). As the Apostle Peter preached one of his sermons he made an appeal that God wants everyone to hear, "Repent ye therefore, and be converted, that your sins may be blotted out, when the times of refreshing shall come from the presence of the Lord" (Acts 3:19 KJV).

Along with true repentance goes *faith in the finished work of Jesus* as the basis of redemption. To the Philippian jailor Paul said, "Believe in the Lord Jesus, and you will be saved" (Acts 16:31). I referred previously to Rom. 1:16 which says that "...the gospel...is the power of God for the salvation of everyone who believes." God saves "those who believe" (I Cor. 1:21). Salvation is "given through faith in Jesus Christ" (Gal. 3:22). The meaning of this saving faith may be seen in Rom. 10:9, 10: "That if you confess with your mouth, 'Jesus is Lord,' and believe in your heart that God raised him from the dead, you will be saved. For it is with your heart that you believe and are justified, and it is with your mouth that you confess and are saved." These verses tell us several things about faith: its object—the risen Savior who conquered death; its sincerity—what you "believe in your heart;" its commitment— "confess with your mouth, 'Jesus is Lord'"; its result— "you...are justified...and saved."

Saving faith rests upon Jesus and Him alone without any dependence on human merit or any "works" that an individual can perform. As seen in the Rom. 10 passage above, saving faith is confirmed by an individual's willingness to confess his trust in Jesus as Savior and to acknowledge that he has made Jesus his Lord.

I learned at my mother's knee that being born in a Christian home did not make me a Christian. I knew that I needed to receive Jesus for myself, for God has no grandchildren. One week before my tenth birthday I had a personal encounter with Jesus Christ in a Friday night revival service in my home church, Poplar Springs Baptist Church. As the congregation stood to sing the closing hymn the pastor stood at the front to receive any who would come acknowledging that they were receiving Jesus as Savior and Lord. I knew that Jesus was knocking at the door of my heart. The Spirit of God convicted me of my need to receive Jesus into my life. As I stepped forward I was saying "yes" to Jesus and asking Him cleanse me of sin and come into my life.

I was redeemed by the Redeemer God has provided. You do not need to be in church to have the same experience.

Dear reader, if you have not been redeemed I pray that what you have read here will be used of God to open your eyes to the truth revealed in Scripture, and that you too will ask Jesus to become your Lord and Savior.

CHAPTER 5

REDEMPTION (Part II)

For he has rescued us from the dominion of darkness and brought us into the kingdom of the Son he loves, in whom we have redemption, the forgiveness of sins. Colossians 1:13, 14.

In this second chapter on redemption it is my purpose to outline many of the blessings that the believer experiences as a result of being redeemed. I will seek to answer two questions: from what is the believer saved? for what is the believer saved?

FROM WHAT IS THE BELIEVER SAVED?

In brief, the person who experiences redemption is saved from the consequences of sin. First, the believer is redeemed from **the moral consequences of sin.** There has been fierce debate concerning what is called "the total depravity" of mankind. This does not mean that unconverted persons are incapable of doing good, but rather that even a person's "good" is tainted by wrong motivation. "The heart is deceitful above all things and beyond cure. Who can understand it?" (Jer. 17:9).

But Jesus redeems the believer from *the wickedness of his heart.* "When God raised up his servant, he sent him first to you to bless you by turning each of you from your wicked ways" (Acts 3:26). "Who gave himself for us to redeem us from all wickedness and to purify for himself a people that are his very own, eager to do what is good" (Titus 2:14).

The moral consequences of sin include an individual's *rebellion against God.* "We all, like sheep, have gone astray, each of us has turned to his own way" (Isa. 53:6a). Our rebellion is remedied by receiving Jesus as Lord and Savior. "For if when we were God's enemies, we were reconciled to him through the death of his Son, how much more, having been reconciled, shall we be saved by his life" (Rom. 5:10).

The Bible teaches the reality of our *personal guilt.* "For whoever keeps the whole law and yet stumbles at just one point is guilty of breaking all of it" (James 2:10). Trusting the Redeemer brings the blessing of having personal guilt removed. "But you know that he appeared so that he might take away our sins" (I John 3:5).

Breaking the moral law of God places us under *a curse.* "Christ redeemed us from the curse of the law by becoming a curse for us, for it is written: 'Cursed is everyone who is hung on a tree'" (Gal. 3:13). Praise God that by receiving the Lord Jesus we exchange the curse for an eternal blessing.

The breaking of God's moral law makes the sinner liable for *judgment,* but the believer's judgment against his sin was borne by Jesus on the cross. "Therefore, there is now no condemnation for those who are in Christ Jesus" (Rom. 8:1).

Sin has produced profound **spiritual consequences.** The believer experiences the blessing of knowing him who is the Light of the World. Jesus declared, "I have come into the world as a light, so that no one who believes in me should stay in darkness" (John 12:46).

Jesus spoke to the *spiritually blind* when He quoted from Isaiah, "You will be ever seeing but never perceiving" (Matt. 13:14). The mission of Jesus included giving sight to the spiritually blind, for He announced, "The Spirit of the Lord..has sent me to proclaim...recovery of sight for the blind" (Luke 4:18, 19). After Jesus restored sight to a man's physical eyes the formerly blind man testified, "One thing I do know. I was blind but now I see!" (John 9:25). This is a testimony that every Christian can give concerning spiritual eyesight.

Sin leaves us *spiritually weak*—too weak to save ourselves, but the strong Son of God does for us what we cannot do for ourselves. "You see, at just the right time, when we were still powerless, Christ died for the ungodly" (Rom. 5:6). The believer can say with Paul, "I can do everything through him who gives me strength" (Phil. 4:13).

Although they may not be able to identify their problem, those outside of Christ are *starving spiritually*. Only Jesus can satisfy the hunger and thirst of their souls. The believer is blessed by partaking of Jesus as the Bread and Water of Life. Jesus asserted, "I am the living bread that came down from heaven. If anyone eats of this bread he will live forever" (John 6:51). Jesus also said, "Whoever drinks the water I give him will never thirst. Indeed, the water I give him will become in him a spring of water welling up to eternal life" (John 4:14).

The condition of a sinner may also be described as *spiritual defilement.* At the Last Supper Jesus said to His disciples, "A person who has had a bath needs only to wash his feet" (John 13:10). Jesus was referring to the spiritual bath that represents a person's conversion when he receives Jesus as Lord and Savior. The dirt of sin has been washed from the soul of the believer.

A person does not usually come to Jesus for salvation until he recognizes that he is *spiritually bankrupt.* Jesus said, "The Spirit of the Lord is on me, because he has anointed me to preach good news to the poor" (Luke 4:18). The spiritual pauper is in greater need than the person who is financially bankrupt. The Good News of the saving power of Jesus is for everyone no matter how deep a person's need may be.

The person outside of Christ is also *spiritually oppressed*, under the spell and power of the Devil. However, Jesus declared that He came "...to release the oppressed" (Luke 4:19). The believer experiences deliverance from Satanic oppression. "The reason the Son of God appeared was to destroy the devil's work" (I John 3:8b).

The blessings of redemption also include being saved from **the mental and emotional consequences of sin**. Sin affects the total being of persons, including the way we think and feel. Jesus was sent to "...bind up the broken hearted" (Isa. 61:1).

Our sinful nature causes us to have a tendency to go to extremes. Some people who are outside of Christ go to the extreme of *legalism*. Legalism tries to make persons good through laws and regulations, not realizing that "Christ is the end of the law so that there may be righteousness for everyone who believes" (Rom. 10:4). Paul warned against a form of legalism in Colosse when he wrote, "Such regulations indeed have an appearance of wisdom, with their self-imposed worship, their false humility and their harsh treatment of the body, but they lack any value in restraining sensual indulgence" (Col. 2:23). Christians should live free of legalism because, "Now that faith has come, we are no longer under the supervision of the law" (Gal. 3:25).

The extreme of *license* is just as deadly. License is the misuse and abuse of freedom. "You, my brothers, were called to be free. But do not use your freedom to indulge the sinful nature" (Gal. 5:13). In his letter to the Romans Paul asks, "Shall we go on sinning so that grace may increase?" Then he answers, "By no means! We died to sin; how can we live in it any longer?" (Rom. 6:1, 2).

Sin leaves persons with a feeling of *emptiness*, but believers find that Jesus fills their lives with meaning and purpose. "For you know that it was not with perishable things such as silver and gold that you were redeemed from the empty way of life handed down to you from your forefathers, but with the precious blood of Christ, a lamb without blemish or defect" (I Peter 1:18, 19). In the place of an "empty way of life," believers claim the promise of Jesus, "I have come that they may have life and have it to the full" (John 10:10).

The believer is also saved from *an accusing conscience*. Paul spoke of "...hypocritical liars, whose consciences have been seared as with a hot iron" (I Tim. 4:2). The way to get rid of an accusing conscience is not by the denial of guilt but by receiving forgiveness through Christ. "How much more, then, will the blood of Christ, who through the eternal Spirit offered himself unblemished to God, cleanse our consciences from acts that lead to death, so that we may serve the living God!" (Heb. 10:14).

Ultimately redemption will provide salvation from **the physical consequences of sin.** When the Bible says, "A man reaps what he sows" (Gal. 6:7), that applies to Christian and non-Christian alike. Christians who smoke get lung cancer at the same rate as the rest of the population. Breaking the moral laws which God incorporated into the universe often affects our physical bodies. David confessed, "My bones have no soundness because of my sin" (Psa. 38:3). This should not be construed to mean that all illness is a direct result of sin. However, in a sense it can be said that all *illness* is an indirect result of Adam's sin.

The Original Sin in the Garden of Eden brought *mortality* and *death* to Adam and his descendants. "Man is destined to die once" (Heb.. 9:27). "For dust you are and to dust you will return" (Gen. 3:19). While living in a mortal body, the believer has an immortal soul that lives on after death. "But God will redeem my life from the grave; he will surely take me to himself" (Psa. 49:15). This redemption has been provided through Christ "...who has destroyed death and has brought life and immortality to light through the gospel" (II Tim. 1:10b). The redemption that takes us to Heaven removes us from the realm of sickness and disease. "There will be no more death or mourning or crying or pain, for the old order of things has passed away" (Rev. 21:4b).

The final stage of redemption will be the renewal of the believer's body through *resurrection*. Then all the effects of sin will be fully removed for eternity. "Then the saying that is written will come true: 'Death has been swallowed up in victory'" (I Cor. 15:54). Later in this book a whole chapter is devoted to the subject of resurrection.

More of the blessings of redemption come into focus as we seek to answer the second question mentioned at the beginning of this chapter.

FOR WHAT IS THE BELIEVER SAVED?

The believer is saved for a life of fellowship with

God. Redemption makes that fellowship possible by giving the believer **the capacity for communion with God**.

"It is because of him that you are in Christ Jesus" (I Cor. 1:30). Being *in Christ* equips us for fellowship with God, for Paul wrote to believers, "You are of Christ, and Christ is of God" (I Cor. 3:23).

The believer can have fellowship with God because "...we were reconciled to him through the death of his Son" (Rom. 5:10). The person who is *reconciled to God* can come into His presence with confidence and assurance.

The believer also experiences the blessing of being *a person who belongs to God*. Jesus "...gave himself for us...to purify for himself a people that are his very own" (Titus 2:14). We who have experienced redemption are "...those who are God's possession" (Eph 1:14). Belonging to God restores the relationship that was broken by sin. How blessed to belong to Him in whose image we were created!

When by redemption we become God's children we possess *the full rights of being His heirs*. "But when the time had fully come, God sent his Son,...that we might receive the full rights of sons" (Gal. 4:4, 5). "Now if we are children, then we are heirs—heirs of God and co-heirs with Christ, if indeed we share in his sufferings in order that we may share in his glory" (Rom. 8:17).

When Jesus died on the cross, "At that moment the curtain of the temple was torn in two from top to bottom" (Matt. 27:50, 51). The way was opened to the Most Holy Place symbolizing the very presence of God. Through Christ's sacrifice of Himself for us *a way of access to the Father* was provided. Through Jesus "...we gained access by faith into this grace in which we now stand" (Rom. 5:2). "For through him we both have access to the Father by one Spirit" (Eph. 2:18). "In him and through faith in him we may approach God with freedom and confidence" (Eph. 3:12). What a blessed promise and precious privilege of coming into the presence of our Heavenly Father!

Jesus declared, "The Spirit of the Lord...has sent me to proclaim freedom for the prisoners" (Luke 4:18). Those outside of Christ are imprisoned by sin, and the worst kind of imprisonment is spiritual. However, the believer is able to fellowship with God in *spiritual freedom.* "So if the Son sets you free you will be free indeed" (John 8:36). "Stand firm then, and do not let yourselves be burdened again by a yoke of slavery" (Gal.5:1).

The believer's fellowship with God will be *for eternity.* Hebrews 9:12 says that Jesus "...obtained eternal redemption" for us through the sacrifice of His blood. Paul spoke of "...the salvation that is in Christ Jesus, with eternal glory" (II Tim. 2:10). "The hour has come for you to wake up from your slumber, because our salvation is nearer now than when we first believed" (Rom. 13:11).

In Christ we not only have the capacity to commune with God; we are also **qualified for communion with God.**

First, the believer is qualified to commune with God because his standing in Christ makes him *blameless* before God. "He will keep you strong to the end, so that you will be blameless on the day of our Lord Jesus Christ" (I Cor. 1:8). In Christ we are blameless because "...the blood of Jesus, his Son, purifies us from all sin" (I John1:7). Believers do sin. "If we claim to be without sin, we deceive ourselves and the truth is not in us" (I John 1:8). When the believer sins it breaks his fellowship with God, but not his relationship to God. Restoration of fellowship and blamelessness is possible, for "If we confess our sins, he is faithful and just and will forgive us our sins and purify us from all unrighteousness" (I John 1:9).

Christ makes it possible for the believer to live *a holy life*. "God...has saved us and called us to a holy life—not because of anything we have done but because of his own purpose and grace. This grace was given us in Christ Jesus before the beginning of time, but it has now been revealed through the appearing of our Savior" (II Tim. 1:8-10). The person who does not desire to live a holy life is giving evidence that he has not been redeemed. "No one who lives in him keeps on sinning" (I John 3:6).

The believer is a person *eager to do what is good*. Paul said that Jesus,"...gave himself for us...to purify for himself a people...eager to do what is good" (Titus 2:15). "For we are God's workmanship created in Christ Jesus to do good works, which God prepared in advance for us to do" (Eph. 2:10).

The believer is also a person *possessing the ability*

to do what is good, an ability that comes from God through His Spirit who dwells in us. "Therefore, my dear friends,...continue to work out your salvation with fear and trembling, for it is God who works in you to will and to act according to his good purpose" (Phil. 2:12, 13).

Believers are qualified for fellowship with God because He provides *the power* to meet His expectations. "But you will receive power when the Holy Spirit comes on you; and you will be my witnesses" (Acts 1:8a). This provision will be discussed further in the chapter on Resources.

Praise God for the redemption that saves believers from the consequences of sin and makes possible an earthly life and an eternity of fellowship with our Father in Heaven!

CHAPTER 6

RIGHTEOUSNESS

I am not ashamed of the gospel, because it is the power of God for the salvation of everyone who believes: first for the Jew, then for the Gentile. For in the gospel a righteousness from God is revealed, a righteousness that is by faith from first to last. Romans 1:16, 17.

One of the principal blessings of redemption is that the believer is made righteous by his relationship to the Redeemer. *The definition of righteousness* depends on the meaning of the word in the original languages of the Bible. Several ideas emerge: moral uprightness, honesty, justice and fulfilled responsibility. Biblical righteousness includes right motivation for actions and unblemished character.

Scripture makes clear *the demand for righteousness.* Righteousness is required for a person to have a relationship with God. In His sermon on the mount Jesus declared, "For I tell you that unless your righteousness surpasses that of the Pharisees and teachers of the law, you will certainly not enter the kingdom of heaven" (Matt. 5:20). Only along "paths of righteousness" (Psa. 23:3), can we experience fellowship with God. Righteousness is also necessary for the believer to be a worthy citizen of God's Kingdom. "For the kingdom of God is not a matter of eating and drinking, but of righteousness, peace and joy in the Holy Spirit" (Rom. 14:17).

In spite of the demand for righteousness, the Scriptures show that there is a complete *dearth of righteousness*. This is taught in both Old and New Testaments, for Romans quotes from Psalms (14:3 and 53:3): "As it is written: 'There is no one righteous, not even one'" (Rom. 3:10). Concerning the natural condition of those who are outside of Christ, the next verse continues, "There is no one who understands, no one who seeks God" (Rom. 3:11).

Those who are outside of Christ may try to be righteous and may take pride in their "goodness." However, the Bible teaches that this is *defective righteousness*. "All of us have become like one who is unclean, and all our righteous acts are like filthy rags" (Isa. 64:6). Those who are outside of Christ do not naturally recognize their true condition before God. "Since they did not know the righteousness that comes from God and sought to establish their own, they did not submit to God's righteousness" (Rom. 10:3).

In the lives of those who persist in going away

from God we see *despised righteousness.* II Peter 2:10 speaks of, "...those who follow the corrupt desire of the sinful nature and despise authority." Consider carefully this description of those who willfully turn away from God: "Furthermore, since they did not think it worthwhile to retain the knowledge of God, he gave them over to a depraved mind, to do what ought not to be done. They became filled with every kind of wickedness, evil, greed and depravity" (Rom. 1:28. 29).

In contrast to this, there was a perfect *demonstration of righteousness* in the life of Jesus. On one occasion He asked His enemies, "Can any of you prove me guilty of sin?" (John 8:46). Paul testified, "For just as through the disobedience of the one man the many were made sinners, so through the obedience of the one man the many will be made righteous" (Rom. 5:19). Jesus is the "one Man" whose obedience to the Father's will was perfect and complete. Jesus claimed concerning the Father's will, "I always do what pleases him" (John 8:29). He also said, "I seek not to please myself but him who sent me" (John 5:30). Jesus lived righteously so that He might offer Himself as a sacrifice for our sin.

If we can "become the righteousness of God," there also will be a demonstration of righteousness in the life of the believer. This is seen in the prayer of Paul: "And this is my prayer:...that you...may be pure and blameless until the day of Christ, filled with the fruit of righteousness that comes through Jesus Christ—to the glory and praise of God" (Phil. 1:9a, 10a&c & 11). Also in Paul's admonition: "Live as children of light (for the fruit of the light consists in all goodness, righteousness and truth)" (Eph. 5:8b, 9).

Righteousness is given to us when the believer is *declared righteous* by God. No one is declared righteous on the basis of any form of human merit. "I do not set aside the grace of God, for if righteousness could be gained through the law, Christ died for nothing!" (Gal. 2:21). We are also told concerning our redemption in Christ, "...he saved us, not because of righteous things we had done, but because of his mercy" (Titus 3:5).

The believer can be declared righteous on the basis of *derived righteousness,* which is received from our perfect Redeemer. "It is because of him [God] that you are in Christ Jesus, who has become for us wisdom from God—that is our righteousness, holiness and redemption" (I Cor. 1:30). "God made him who had no sin to be sin for us, so that we might become the righteousness of God" (II Cor. 5:21).

A minister was at the bedside of a dying man. He asked, "Sandy, would you tell me how you were converted?"

Sandy replied, "When I was sixty years of age the Lord Jesus came along and said to me, 'Sandy, I'll exchange you.'"

"Exchange, Sandy; and what did you give him?"

"I gave him all my years of sin and my sinful heart, and he gave me in return his righteousness."

Our sin was placed on Jesus so that His righteousness might be placed in us.

In theological terms it is said that righteousness

is "imputed" to the believer. This means that *a deposit of righteousness* is credited to the believer. "To the man who does not work but trusts God who justifies the wicked, his faith is credited as righteousness" (Rom. 4:5). When a person has a line of credit in a bank, there is a limited amount available. But that is not true of the believer's line of credit in the bank of Heaven. Jesus not only paid my sin debt and that of the whole world; His perfect righteousness is credited to me since I trusted Him as Savior and received Him as Lord.

Paul cites Abraham as an example of one who was made righteous by faith even in Old Testament times. "What does the Scripture say? 'Abraham believed God, and it was credited to him as righteousness" (Rom. 4:3). Later in the same chapter Paul explains further, "The words 'it was credited to him' were written not for him alone, but also for us, to whom God will credit righteousness—for us who believe in him who raised Jesus our Lord from the dead" (Rom.4:23, 24). The believer is wealthy in Christ, able to draw upon an account of unlimited righteousness.

Righteousness is deposited to the account of those who allow God to find them. "What then shall we say? That the Gentiles, who did not pursue righteousness, have attained it" (Rom. 9:30). When a person allows "the Hound of Heaven" to overtake him, he discovers that he has "attained" righteousness by faith.

The desire for righteousness is natural for the person who is in Christ. "Blessed are those who hunger and thirst for righteousness, for they shall be filled" (Matt. 5:6). The believer who is in fellowship with God will want to fulfill the challenge, "Do not offer the parts of your body to sin, as instruments of wickedness, but rather offer yourselves to God, as those who have been brought from death to life; and offer the parts of your body to him as instruments of righteousness" (Rom. 6:13). The believer desires to be "enslaved" by righteousness rather than by sin. "You have been set free from sin and have become slaves of righteousness" (Rom. 6:18). This is a liberating enslavement. The believer is free to become what God created him to be. Sin's chains have been broken. Righteousness is expressed in the life when the indwelling Christ is allowed to express Himself through the believer.

When we "...grow in grace and knowledge of our Lord and Savior Jesus Christ" (II Peter 3:18), there is *a deepening righteousness* in the life of the believer. Scripture tells us, God "...will enlarge the harvest of your righteousness" (II Cor. 9:10). God uses a number of things to promote righteousness in the lives of His children. One thing He uses is His Word. Jesus said, "You are already clean because of the word I have spoken to you" (John 15:3).

God also uses trials and suffering to help develop the believer's righteousness. "Consider it pure joy, my brothers, whenever you face trials of many kinds, because you know that the testing of your faith develops perseverance. Perseverance must finish its work so that you may be mature and complete, not lacking anything" (James 1:2-4).

Righteousness in the believer's life is deepened through the work of the Holy Spirit. "And so he [Jesus] condemned sin in sinful man, in order that the righteous requirements of the law might be fully met in us, who do not live according to the sinful nature but according to the Spirit" (Rom. 8:3b, 4). The believer lives "according to the Spirit" when he depends on the Holy Spirit as his source of strength to live righteously and when he is available to the Holy Spirit as an instrument of ministry to persons for whom Christ died. In the early part of this chapter I cited Romans 14:17 where it tells us that "the kingdom of God is...a matter of...righteousness...in the Holy Spirit."

I close with the words of the prophet Hosea, "...it is time to seek the Lord, until he comes and showers righteousness on you" (Hosea 10:12).

CHAPTER 7

RESOURCES

Grace and peace be yours in abundance through the knowledge of God and of Jesus our Lord. His divine power has given us everything we need for life and godliness through our knowledge of him who called us by his own glory and goodness. 2 Peter 1:2, 3.

T he believer's spiritual blessings include "everything we need for life and godliness." We can live in robust spiritual health when we properly avail ourselves of the resources belonging to all who know Jesus as personal Savior and Lord. Our resources include:

THE PRESENCE OF THE SAVIOR

Jesus *promised* His presence to His followers. "And surely I am with you always, to the very end of the age" (Matt. 28:20b). Another assurance of the Savior's presence is found in these words: "When you were dead in your sins and in the uncircumcision of your sinful nature, God made you alive with Christ" (Col. 2:13). What a blessing to be made "alive with Christ!"

Although Jesus is present at all times with every believer through the indwelling Holy Spirit, there is a sense in which His presence must be *procured* daily. To have Christ's presence as an enabling power for our Christian walk, we must accept the fact of our positional death with Christ. The believer can testify, "I have been crucified with Christ and I no longer live, but Christ lives in me" (Gal. 2:20). This is also stated in the following words: "For you died, and your life is now hidden with Christ in God" (Col. 3:3). This means that by faith we deny ourselves and rely on the indwelling Christ to live through us. "I pray that out of his glorious riches he may strengthen you with power through his Spirit in your inner being, so that Christ may dwell in your hearts through faith" (Eph. 3:16, 17).

The presence of Jesus is procured as we continue to walk in fellowship with Him. "So then, just as you received Christ Jesus as Lord, continue to live in him, rooted and built up in him, strengthened in the faith, as you were taught, and overflowing with thankfulness" (Col 2:6, 7). We must faithfully follow Him by doing His will daily, for He said, "My sheep listen to my voice; I know them, and they follow me" (John 10:27).

The presence of Jesus may also be *perceived.*

What a blessing it is to have a conscious realization of His presence. This blessing was promised by Jesus Himself: "On that day you will realize that I am in my Father, and you are in me, and I am in you" (John 14:20). The spiritual presence of Jesus is just as real as His physical presence was on the day of His resurrection when He walked with two disciples on the road to Emmaus. Along with them we will sometimes realize His presence with burning hearts. "They asked each other, 'Were not our hearts burning within us while he talked with us in the road and opened the Scriptures to us?" (Luke 24:32).

The perceived presence of the Savior will be a conscious realization only as long as we live in obedience to all we understand of His will. Jesus clearly stated that condition when He promised: "Whoever has my commands and obeys them, he is the one who loves me. He who loves me will be loved by my Father, and I too will love him and show myself to him" (John 14:21). Jesus enlarged on the promise by adding, "If anyone loves me he will obey my teaching. My Father will love him, and we will come to him and make our home with him" (John 14:23). The believer can experience no greater blessing than to have conscious fellowship with his Father and Elder Brother.

Another important resource for the believer is:

THE POWER OF THE SPIRIT

The power of God's Spirit is essential to our

sanctification, to our being set apart to God as His exclusive possession. After Paul described the sinful lifestyle of many in Corinth, he said, "And this is what some of you were. But you were washed, you were sanctified, you were justified in the name of the Lord Jesus Christ and by the Spirit of our God" (I Cor. 6:11). Peter described "God's elect" (I Peter 1:1) as those "...who have been chosen according to the foreknowledge of God, through the sanctifying work of the Spirit" (I Peter 1:2a). The Holy Spirit makes the believer a part of Christ's Body, the Church, and enables the believer to grow in his relationship to Christ.

The believer's *security* in Christ is guaranteed by the power of the Spirit. "Now it is God who makes both us and you stand firm in Christ. He anointed us, and put his Spirit in our hearts as a deposit guaranteeing what is to come" (II Cor. 1:21, 22). Paul amplified that thought when he said that the Holy Spirit, "...is a deposit guaranteeing our inheritance until the redemption of those who are God's possession" (Eph. 1:14). How secure we are in Christ when the Holy Spirit guarantees our inheritance of all the blessings of Heaven!

The Holy Spirit also provides our *satisfaction* as believers. This is my understanding of the meaning of the words of Jesus to the woman at the well near Sychar: "Everyone who drinks this water will thirst again, but whoever drinks the water I give him will never thirst. Indeed, the water I give him will become in him a spring of water welling up to eternal life" (John 4:13, 14). Several times the New

Testament uses water as a symbol of the Holy Spirit, as I believe Jesus does here.

The power of the Spirit is the source of the believer's spiritual *strength*. This is the implication of Paul's prayer: "I pray that out of his glorious riches he may strengthen you with power through his Spirit in your inner being" (Eph. 3:16). Paul also wrote, "For when I am weak, then I am strong" (II Cor. 12:10). Only when we realize our weakness will we depend on the strength that can come only from the Holy Spirit.

The power of the Spirit is needed for Christian *service*. "'Not by might nor by power, but by my Spirit,' says the Lord Almighty" (Zech. 4:6b). Only as the believer is empowered by the Holy Spirit can he obey the admonition: "Never be lacking in zeal, but keep your spiritual fervor, serving the Lord" (Rom. 12:11).

The Spirit's power is essential for *soul winning*. Jesus said, "But you will receive power when the Holy Spirit comes on you; and you will be my witnesses in Jerusalem, and in all Judea and Samaria, and to the ends of the earth" (Acts 1:8). The early believers were used of God in this ministry of evangelizing unbelievers when, "All of them were filled with the Holy Spirit..." (Acts 2:4a). To be filled with the Spirit is to be under His control and empowered for the witness Jesus has commissioned us to give by sharing the Gospel "to the ends of the earth."

Being filled with the Spirit causes the believer to express the fruit of the Spirit through spiritual *singing*. "Do not get drunk on wine, which leads to debauchery. Instead, be filled with the Spirit. Speak to one another with psalms, hymns and spiritual songs. Sing and make music in your heart to the Lord" (Eph. 5:18, 19).

The Holy Spirit is a constant internal resource for all believers. What a blessing to be indwelled by Him of whom it is written, "...the one who is in you is greater than the one who is in the world" (I John 4:4b). Praise God that He is stronger than the Evil One who is in the world.

THE PRAYER OF SUPPLICATION

Prayer is a great privilege and a powerful resource available to all believers. One of the great prayer promises says, "The prayer of a righteous man is powerful and effective" (James 5:16b). The previous chapter on Righteousness shows that this is a promise applying to all Christians who are in a right standing with the Heavenly Father.

Sometimes a right standing with God requires that our prayer begin with confession of any sin that has broken our fellowship with Him. Through prayer we may ask *for pardon*. Surely we ask with the prophet, "Who is a God like you, who pardons sin? (Micah 7:18a). Yet that is what God promises to do as we make honest confession.

Having confessed our sins, we may pray *for purity* of life in the future. "Therefore, I urge you, brothers, in view of God's mercy, to offer your bodies as living sacrifices, holy and pleasing to God—this is your spiritual act of worship" (Rom. 12:1).

We may pray confidently *for peace* of mind and heart. "Do not be anxious about anything, but in everything, by prayer and petition, with thanksgiving, present your requests to God. And the peace of God which transcends all understanding, will guard your hearts and your minds in Christ Jesus" (Phil. 4:4).

Thank God we may ask *for patience*. We may pray for others and for ourselves as Paul prayed for the Colossians: "...being strengthened with all power according to his glorious might so that you may have great endurance and patience" (Col. 1:11).

Closely related to patience is the prayer *for perseverance*. "You need to persevere so that when you have done the will of God, you will receive what he promised" (Heb. 10:36). The Letter of James also emphasized the importance of the believer persevering in his Christian walk: "Perseverance must finish its work so that you may be mature and complete, not lacking anything" (James 1:4).

The believer may pray *for prosperity* that will glorify the Lord. When we meditate daily on God's Word, we may claim the promise: "He is like a tree planted by streams of water, which yields its fruit in season and whose leaf does not wither. Whatever he does prospers" (Psa. 1:3).

THE PROMISES OF SCRIPTURE

We can be thankful for the *plentitude* of Bible promises. This must have been in the mind of the psalmist when he wrote: "Many, O Lord my God, are thy thoughts which are to us-ward; they cannot be reckoned up in order unto thee: if I would declare and speak them, they are more than can be numbered" (Psa. 40:5 KJV).

The promises of Scripture are *precious.* "Through these he has given us his very great and precious promises, so that through them you may participate in the divine nature and escape the corruption in the world caused by evil desires" (II Peter 1:4).

We can rejoice in the *purpose* stated in the promise, "And God is able to make all grace abound to you, so that in all things at all times, having all you need, you will abound in every good work" (II Cor. 9:8).

We may depend on the promises of Scripture because of their *perfection.* "Every good and perfect gift is from above, coming down from the Father of the heavenly lights, who does not change like shifting shadows" (James 1:17).

Bible promises are also dependable because of their *permanence.* "Your word, O Lord, is eternal; it stands firm in the heavens" (Psa. 119:89).

The promises of Scripture are an important resource because of their *profit,* because they are profitable in all areas of the believer's life. This thought is supported by the following words of the psalmist: "I rejoice in your promise, like one who finds great spoil" (Psa. 119:16); "By them is your servant warned; in keeping them there is great reward" (Psa. 19:11).

Some Bible promises become a great blessing as

we claim them according to our daily needs. In the great Faith chapter, Hebrews 11, there is a list of some of the great accomplishments of faith. Verse 33 speaks of those, "...who through faith subdued kingdoms, wrought righteousness, obtained promises, stopped the mouths of lions." We along with them may partake of God's promises by faith.

PARTAKING OF SCRIPTURE

In the chapter on Revelation we presented Scripture as a most important medium of God's communication with His Creatures. Attention was given to the different ways persons respond to Scripture. Believers respond positively to God's message. A sterling example of this is seen in the following verse: "And we thank God continually because, when you received the word of God, which you heard from us, you accepted it not as the word of men, but as it actually is, the word of God, which is at work in you who believe" (I Thess. 2:13).

Individuals become Christian believers by partaking of Scripture for *salvation*. Paul wrote to Timothy, "...from infancy you have known the holy Scriptures, which are able to make you wise for salvation through faith in Christ Jesus" (II Tim. 3:15). God's written Word is our dependable source of knowledge about His Living Word, the Savior. To come to know Him through Scripture made alive by God's Spirit is to experience salvation.

Having been saved, we need to partake of Scripture daily for *spiritual strength*. The Bible tells us that some of the great heroes of faith, "...quenched the fury of the flames, and escaped the edge of the sword; whose weakness was changed to strength" (Heb. 11:34a). God's Word can strengthen us against temptation, for the psalmist asserted, "I Have hidden your word in my heart that I might not sin against you" (Psa. 119:11).

Scripture provides strength to believers because it is the source of *spiritual food*, nourishment for our souls: "...man does not live on bread alone but on every word that comes from the mouth of the Lord" (Deut. 8:3). Believers are admonished: "Like newborn babies, crave pure spiritual milk, so that by it you may grow up in your salvation, now that you have tasted that the Lord is good" (I Peter 2:2). The Bible provides nourishing spiritual "milk" that is essential to Christian growth. Every believer should be able to testify with Job, "I have treasured the words of his mouth more than my daily bread" (Job 23:12b).

A proper intake of Scripture should lead to growth into *spiritual maturity*. "All Scripture is God-breathed and is useful for teaching, rebuking, correcting and training in righteousness, so that the man of God may be thoroughly equipped for every good work" (II Tim. 3:16, 17).

Believers gladly partake of Scripture because of its *sweetness*, saying with the Psalmist, "How sweet are your promises to my taste, sweeter than honey to my mouth!" (Psa. 119:103). On one occasion the prophet Jeremiah said to God, "When your words came, I ate them; they were my joy and my heart's delight" (Jer. 15:16).

We partake of Scripture by the *study* of the Bible. "Do your best to present yourself to God, as one approved, a workman who does not need to be ashamed and who correctly handles the word of truth" (II Tim 2:15). Only by diligent Spirit-led study can you be one "who correctly handles the word of truth."

Our partaking of Scripture is aided by the kind of *supplication* made by the psalmist when he prayed, "Open my eyes that I may see wonderful things in your law" (Psa. 119:18). We would also do well to pray, "Oh, that my ways were steadfast in obeying your decrees!" (Psa. 119:5). May a good spiritual appetite motivate us to feed on God's Word daily.

THE PREACHING OF SCRIPTURE

We are told that when Jesus "ascended on high" He "...gave gifts to men" (Eph. 4:8). Verse 11 of the same chapter lists some leaders whom Jesus has given to the Church: "...he gave some to be apostles, some to be prophets, some to be evangelists, and some to be pastors and teachers." An important resource to believers is the preaching of Scripture that they can hear week-by-week in times of worship with other believers. If at all possible, this needs to be more than preaching heard on radio or television. It needs to be preaching by a godly pastor in a local church that is following the New Testament pattern.

Such a pastor will be a true *messenger of God's Word* who can say with the Apostle Paul, "...when I preach the gospel, I cannot boast, for I am compelled to preach" (I Cor. 9:16a). He will be a pastor who follows the example of Paul when he declared, "For we do not preach ourselves, but Jesus Christ as Lord" (II Cor. 4:5a). Concerning the preaching of such a pastor, it can be said, "How beautiful are the feet of those who bring good news!" (Rom. 10:15b).

If the pastor's preaching is truly *the ministry of God's Word* to his hearers, he will be able to say with Jesus, "The Spirit of the Lord is on me, because he has anointed me to preach good news to the poor" (Luke 4:18a).

The worthy pastor's preaching will share *the message of the Gospel* as it was shared by Paul in Thessalonica: "...he reasoned with them from the Scriptures, explaining and proving that the Christ had to suffer and rise from the dead" (Acts 17:2b & 3a). Concerning those who need to hear the Gospel, we may ask, "How can they hear without someone preaching to them?" (Rom. 10:14b).

The preaching of Scripture is a blessing to believers when it makes clear *the meaning of God's Word.* Every pastor needs to remember Paul's charge to Timothy, "Preach the Word; be prepared in season and out of season; correct, rebuke and encourage— with great patience and careful instruction" (II Tim. 4:2). The pastor can make no more important prayer request than this: "Pray also for me, that whenever I open my mouth, words may be given me so that I will fearlessly make known the mystery of the gospel" (Eph. 6:19). Thank God if you have a pastor who faithfully "breaks the bread of life."

PARTICIPATION WITH THE SAINTS

An important resource for believers is their fellowship with other members of God's Family on earth. We are admonished to make this a regular part of our lives. "Let us not give up meeting together, as some are in the habit of doing, but let us encourage one another—and all the more as you see the Day approaching" (Heb. 10:25). The approaching "Day" of worship should not be neglected by any believer.

This means regular participation with other Christians *in the worship of God*. The challenge issued by the psalmist, "Come, let us bow down in worship, let us kneel before the Lord our Maker" (Psa. 95:6), applies equally to New Testament believers. Our times of private worship do not negate our need for worship with fellow believers.

Believers participate with one another *in waiting upon God*. "Blessed are all who wait for him" (Isa. 30:18c). Sometimes we need to wait for God to help us discern the message of His Word. "I wait for the Lord, my soul waits, and in his word I put my hope" (Psa. 130:5). We sometimes have to wait upon God to discover His will. In such cases the problem is with us, not with Him. When we want things contrary to God's will, waiting on Him gives God opportunity to change our desires. We can wait for God with confidence, anticipating what He will do. "My soul waits for the Lord more than watchmen wait for the morning" (Psa. 130:6a).

We are sometimes in a hurry, but God never is. Waiting for Him helps us to learn patience. "Be still before the Lord and wait patiently for him" (Psa. 37:7a).

In the fellowship of a local church it is possible for believers to run ahead of God and to think they are doing the work of God when He is not working through them. The psalmist wrote, "As the eyes of slaves look to the hand of their master, ...so our eyes look to the Lord our God" (Psa. 123:2a & c). Believers need to wait upon God until they see where He is at work and where He wants them to join Him in Christian ministry.

Believers participate *in working with the Lord*. "For we are God's fellow workers" (I Cor. 3:9a). "As God's fellow workers we urge you not to receive God's grace in vain" (II Cor. 6:1). Working together in Christian ministry requires a common Lord, a common sharing of the load and a common love for the Lord and for the lost.

Our Christian fellowship includes *walking in love*. Jesus declared, "By this all men will know that you are my disciples, if you love one another" (John 13:35). Is this evidence of discipleship being manifested in our lifestyle every day? "And let us consider how we may spur one another on toward love and good deeds" (Heb. 10:24)).

Christians share in *witness to the world*. All four Gospels and the book of Acts have some form of the "Great Commission" of Jesus. It makes witness to the world the primary task of the Church. Jesus said, "For the Son of Man came to seek and to save what was lost" (Luke 19:10). He also said, "As the Father sent me, I am sending you" (John 20:21b). As the task of bearing witness to Jesus is shared by fellow believers the load is made lighter and the effectiveness of the witness is multiplied.

Finally, believers share in *warring against evil*. "For our struggle is not against flesh and blood, but against the rulers, against the authorities, against the powers of this dark world and against the spiritual forces of evil in the heavenly realms" (Eph. 6:12). In this spiritual warfare with the devil and the demonic forces of evil, believers do not fight <u>for</u> victory but <u>from</u> victory, enforcing the victory that Jesus won in our behalf when by His death and resurrection He "bruised the head of the Serpent" (see Gen. 3:15). There is a more detailed look at this victory in the chapter on Reigning.

CHAPTER 8

REIGNING

For if, by the trespass of the one man, death reigned through that one man, how much more will those who receive God's abundant provision of grace and of the gift of righteousness reign in life through the one man, Jesus Christ (Rom. 5:17).

In the previous chapter we read of the resources available to those who are "in Christ." The right use of those resources enables a person to "reign in life," which is the believer's birthright. The Bible has a number of references to reigning and to victory, yet too many professing Christians are not living a life of victory. As we examine this subject in Scripture, it is my prayer that a number of readers will have a deeper experience of reigning in life.

The Scripture verse quoted above leads me to think first of **the believer's past.** The "trespass" mentioned is the sin of Adam in the Garden Of Eden. Since the Original Sin "death reigned" for all persons on earth. This is part of the believer's past. We inherited a sinful nature from Adam, and we inherited a mortal body that begins to die as soon as it is born. This Subject was considered in the chapters on Redemption.

The believer's position is described as, "…those who receive God's abundant provision of grace and of the gift of righteousness." By receiving Jesus into his life as Lord and Savior, the believer becomes a partaker of God's grace. In spite of the believer having been a sinner by nature and choice, "where sin abounded, grace did much more abound" (Rom. 5:20b KJV).

In the Gospel of John we note that now after having received God's grace, the believer is "born again" (3:3) and "born of the Spirit" (3:8), has "eternal life" (3:16), is a partaker of "Living Water" (4:10) and of "Living Bread" (6:51), follows "the Light of the World" (8:12), knows "the Truth" and is "set free" (8:32), has come into God's Sheepfold by "the Gate" (10:7) and is following "the Good Shepherd" (10:11). Furthermore, the believer has life "to the full" (10:10), will "never perish" (10:28), knows Him who is "the Way, the Truth and the Life" (14:6), is a branch on "the True Vine" (15:5), has Jesus as his "Friend" (15:13) and is being guided by the Spirit "into all truth" (16:13).

In Romans we learn that the believer's position also includes: having been "called to belong to Jesus Christ" (1:6), and "called to be saints" (1:7); having "faith in Jesus" (3:26), being "justified" (3:28) and "forgiven" (4:7); having "peace" (5:1) and "the hope" of sharing "the glory of God" (5:2); being "saved from God's wrath" (5:9); "no longer slaves of sin" (6:6); "alive to God in Jesus Christ (6:11); "not under law but under grace" (6:14); serving "in the new way of the Spirit" (7:6); under "no condemnation" (8:1); "controlled...by the Spirit" (8:9); "predestined to be conformed to the likeness of his [God's] Son" (8:29); assured that nothing can "separate us from the love of God that is in Christ Jesus our Lord" (8:39). We could go on and on, but I will not attempt an exhaustive examination of this theme. I believe the paragraphs above show that the believer's position in Christ is the basis for a person being able to "reign in life."

However, **a believer's present** may not be a consistent experience of reigning because of some of *the problems that can prevent victory.* One is the downward pull of our human nature. Paul wrote about this: "I do not understand what I do. For what I want to do I do not do, but what I hate I do. ...I know that nothing good lives in me, that is in my sinful nature. For I have the desire to do what is good, but I cannot carry it out" (Rom. 7:15 & 18). That is a struggle with which each of us can identify.

Another problem that can prevent victory is pride. "But he gives more grace. That is why Scripture says: 'God opposes the proud but gives grace to the humble" (James 4:8). Pride of race, place, face or grace can block the flow of God's grace into our lives, grace that enables us to be victorious. For this problem of pride Scripture calls us to humble ourselves. "Humble yourselves before the Lord, and he will lift you up" (James 4:10).

Pride can prevent us from confessing our sins. And failure to confess sins to God blocks His blessings. The psalmist said concerning his prayer, "If I had cherished sin in my heart, the Lord would not have listened" (Psa. 66:18). Another Psalm says, "The eyes of the Lord are on the righteous and his ears are attentive to their cry; the face of the Lord is against those who do evil" (34:15, 16a). Isaiah wrote, "...your sins have hidden his [God's] face from you, so that he will not hear" (Isa. 59:2b). Christians who are out of fellowship with God cannot experience victory. However, when we regularly confess our sins to God, we will be able to say with the psalmist, "I said, 'I will confess my transgressions to the Lord'—and you forgave the guilt of my sin" (Psa. 32:5b).

Another cause of defeat is a spirit of unforgiveness. Jesus warned, "But if you do not forgive men their sins, your Father will not forgive your sins" (Matt. 6:15). In the Model Prayer Jesus taught us to pray, "Forgive us our debts, as we also have forgiven our debtors" (Matt. 6:12).

Christians will not live in victory as long as they refuse to fully obey the will of God. When God called Moses to return to Egypt to lead the Israelites out of slavery, his final excuse for not obeying was expressed in these words, "O Lord, please send someone else to do it" (Exodus 4:13). The next verse says, "Then the Lord's anger burned against Moses."

To Moses' credit he did finally obey. God promises, "Obey me, and I will be your God and you will be my people" (Jer. 7:23).

In spite of the problems preventing victory there are a number of *promises assuring victory.* We are promised victory over the world. Jesus declared, "In the world you will have trouble. But take heart! I have overcome the world" (John 16:33b). Our faith in Jesus enables us to participate in His victory. "This is the victory that has overcome the world, even our faith. Who is it that overcomes the world? Only he who believes that Jesus is the Son of God" (1 John 4:4b, 5).

Although Paul struggled with the downward pull of his human nature he experienced victory: "What a wretched man I am! Who will rescue me from this body of death? Thanks be to God—through Jesus Christ our Lord! (Rom. 7:24, 25). We too may claim the promise of victory through Jesus when He is our Lord. Paul repeated the promise: "But thanks be to God! He gives us the victory through our Lord Jesus Christ" (1 Cor. 15:57).

Believers are promised victory over the trials and tribulations of life. "Who shall separate us from the love of Christ? Shall trouble or hardship or persecution or famine or nakedness or danger or sword? No, in all these things we are more than conquerors through him who loved us" (Rom. 8:35 & 37). The blessing of being "more than conquerors" is ours because of the love our Savior has for each and every believer.

As the promises above would indicate, the

believer can "reign in life" through *the Person providing victory*—the Lord Jesus Christ. "For he must reign until he has put all enemies under his feet" (I Cor. 15:25). Jesus reigns now at the right hand of the Father—the place of honor and authority.

The believer reigns when Jesus reigns on the throne of his heart. Paul testified, "I die every day" (1 Cor. 15:31a). Every believer must die to self to give Jesus the rightful place in his life. Jesus declared, "If anyone would come after me, he must deny himself and take up his cross daily and follow me" (Luke 9:23). But how do we do this? The answer is found in another testimony from Paul: "I have been crucified with Christ and I no longer live but Christ lives in me. The life I live in the body, I live by faith in the Son of God, who loved me and gave himself for me" (Gal. 2:20). A gospel song asks the question, "Were you there when they crucified my Lord?" In a spiritual sense every believer was on the cross with Jesus. By faith the believer can accept the fact that he died with Christ and was raised to new life in Christ. We who know Jesus can begin each day by asking Him to take the throne of our lives for that day and to live His life through us. The victorious believer is one who faithfully follows Jesus in ministry and witness to the world. The believer's life is to be a continuing incarnation of Jesus in the world so that he can say, "I no longer live, but Christ lives."

Reigning is also **the believer's prospect.** We have the prospect of *Reigning with Jesus.* "Here is a trustworthy saying: If we died with him, we will also live with him; if we endure, we will also reign with him" (2 Tim. 2:11, 12a)

After death or after the return of Jesus, which ever occurs first, believers will share in His *reign on earth.* "You have made them to be a kingdom of priests to serve our God, and they will reign on the earth" (Rev. 5:10). Further on in Revelation we learn that this reigning will be for a millennium: "The second death has no power over them, but they will be priests of God and of Christ and will reign with him for a thousand years" (Rev. 20:6).

But that will not end the reigning of believers. "And they will reign for ever and ever" (Rev. 22:5c).

Those of us who have eternal life through Jesus Christ "reign in life" and continue to reign beyond physical death. Early in the chapter I spoke of this as the believer's "birthright." We have been born into God's forever family. May we live as children of the King!

CHAPTER 9

RESURRECTION

*But Christ has indeed been raised from the
dead, the firstfruits of them that have fallen
asleep. For since death came through a man,
the resurrection of the dead also comes
through a man (1 Cor. 15:20,21).*

Believers, like the unsaved, live in mortal bodies
that will die and return to the dust from which
God created Adam. But because believers have eternal life, they look forward to the great blessing of
having their bodies raised from death. In this chapter
I will try to present what I understand the Bible to
teach about the blessing of resurrection.

AFFIRMATIONS OF THE BLESSING
OF RESURRECTION

The believer's hope of being raised is stated in

many Scripture passages. The most ancient affirmation of belief in the resurrection is probably *the one made by Job*: "And after my skin has been destroyed, yet in my flesh I will see God; I myself will see him with my own eyes" (Job 19:26, 27). What a blessing will be ours to have a resurrection body that can live in the presence of God!

Jesus taught that even *Moses* affirmed belief in the believer's resurrection. This we see in the following words of Jesus, "But in the account of the bush, even Moses showed that the dead rise, for he calls the Lord 'the God of Abraham, and the God of Isaac, and the God Jacob.' He is not the God of the dead, but the God of the living, for to him all are alive" (Luke 20:37, 38).

When Jesus came to the home of Mary and Martha after the death of their brother Lazarus, *Martha* affirmed her belief in the resurrection of the brother, "I know he will rise again in the resurrection at the last day" (John 11:24).

The blessing of our bodies being raised is also attested by the *resurrections* that took place *at the time of the death of Jesus* on the cross. "The tombs broke open and the bodies of many holy people who had died were raised to life. They came out of the tombs; and after Jesus' resurrection they went into the holy city and appeared to many people" (Matt. 27:52, 53).

The *preaching of the Apostles* gave witness to the fact that believers can look forward to the blessing of resurrection. "But if it is preached that Christ has been raised from the dead, how can some of you say that there is no resurrection from the dead?" (I Cor. 15:12).

The most important affirmations of resurrection are those made by *Jesus*. He declared, "And this the will of him who sent me, that I shall lose none of all that he has given me, but raise them up in the last day" (John 3:39).

ASSURANCES OF THE BLESSING OF RESURRECTION

The believer's resurrection is not only affirmed, it is also assured by *the resurrection of Jesus*. "But Christ has indeed been raised from the dead, the first fruits of those who have fallen asleep" (1 Cor. 15:20).

Believers know that the blessing of resurrection is certain because of *the saving power of Jesus*. Before He called Lazarus from the tomb, Jesus said, "I am the resurrection and the life. He who believes in me will live even though he dies" (John 11:25). To "believe in" Jesus is to receive Him as personal Savior and Lord, as we saw in earlier chapters. Jesus promises to raise the bodies of those who believe in Him. "For my Father's will is that everyone who looks to the Son and believes in him shall have eternal life, and I will raise him up at the last day" (John 6:40).

When a person receives Jesus as Savior and Lord, He comes by His Spirit to live in that person's life. *The Spirit's indwelling presence* assures the believer of the future resurrection of his body.

"Now it is God who has made us for this very purpose [to be clothed with immortality] and has given us the Spirit as a deposit guaranteeing what is to come" (II Cor. 5:5).

THE ACCOMPLISHMENT OF THE BLESSING OF RESURRECTION

All three Persons of the triune Godhead are involved in the accomplishment of the believer's resurrection. *God the Father* is mentioned in I Cor. 6:14, "By his power God raised the Lord Jesus from the dead, and he will raise us also."

The believer's resurrection is also said to be accomplished by *God the Son*. "But our citizenship is in heaven. And we eagerly await a Savior from there, the Lord Jesus Christ, who by the power that enables him to bring everything under his control, will transform our lowly bodies so that they will be like his glorious body" (Phil. 3:20, 21).

The resurrection of the body is also the work of *the Holy Spirit*, the third Person of the Trinity. "And if the Spirit of him who raised Jesus from the dead is living in you, he who raised Christ from the dead, will also give life to your mortal bodies through his Spirit who lives in you" (Rom. 8:11).

The resurrection will be accomplished *when Jesus returns* to receive His own. "But each in his own turn: Christ the firstfruits; then when he comes, those who belong to him" (I Cor. 15:23).

THE ANTICIPATION OF THE BLESSING OF RESURRECTION

The blessing of resurrection is eagerly anticipated by spiritual believers. It is anticipated as both *a personal and universal blessing.* "We know that the whole creation has been groaning as in the pains of childbirth right up to the present time. Not only so, but we ourselves who have the firstfruits of the Spirit, groan inwardly as we wait eagerly for our adoption as sons, the redemption of our bodies" (Rom. 8:22, 23). This anticipation is *a comforting hope* for believers. "Therefore encourage each other with these words" (I Thess. 4:18).

It is also *a purifying hope.* "For the grace of God that brings salvation has appeared to all men. It teaches us to say 'No' to ungodliness and worldly passions, and to live self-controlled, upright and godly lives in this present age, while we wait for the blessed hope—the glorious appearing of our great God and Savior, Jesus Christ, who gave himself for us to redeem us from all wickedness and to purify for himself a people that are his very own, eager to do what is good" (Titus 2:11-14). Anticipating the return of Jesus to either transform or resurrect our bodies, motivates believers "to live self-controlled, upright and godly lives."

THINGS THAT ACCOMPANY THE BLESSING OF RESURRECTION

The resurrection of believers at the return of

Jesus will be accompanied by *the shout of Jesus, the summons of the archangel* and *the sounding of God's trumpet.* These are all mentioned in I Thess. 4:14-17, "We believe that Jesus died and rose again, and so we believe that God will bring with Jesus those who have fallen asleep in him. According to the Lord's own word, we tell you that we who are still alive, who are left till the coming of the Lord, will certainly not precede those who have fallen asleep. For the Lord himself will come down from heaven, with a loud command, with the voice of the archangel and with the trumpet call of God, and the dead in Christ will rise first. After that we who are still alive and are left will be caught up together with them in the clouds to meet the Lord in the air. And so we will be with the Lord forever."

The shout of Jesus was also mentioned by Him as he talked about the resurrection. "Do not be amazed at this, for a time is coming when all who are in the graves will hear his voice and come out— those who have done good will rise to live, and those who have done evil will rise to be condemned" (John 5:28, 29). Resurrection will be a blessing only for believers. However, the resurrection of the righteous and wicked will be separated by the millennial reign of Jesus on earth.

Another reference to the sounding of God's trumpet is found in I Cor. 15:51-53, "Listen, I tell you a mystery: we will not all sleep, but we will all be changed. For the trumpet will sound, the dead will be raised imperishable, and we will be changed."

THINGS ASSOCIATED WITH THE BLESSING OF RESURRECTION

The resurrection of believers will be associated with several events that make resurrection a great blessing. One is *the destruction of death.* I Cor. 15:25 & 26 says of Jesus, "For he must reign until he has put all enemies under his feet. The last enemy to be destroyed is death." Further on that chapter says, "When the perishable has been clothed with the imperishable, and the mortal with immortality, then the saying that is written will come true: 'Death has been swallowed up in victory'" (I Cor. 15:54). In eternity there will be no funerals and no bereavement or sorrow of any kind.

The resurrection will mean that believers will live in *transformed bodies* that are no longer hampered by the limitations of earth. "The body that is sown is perishable, it is raised imperishable; is it sown in dishonor, it is raised in glory; it is sown in weakness, it is raised in power; it is sown a natural body, it is raised a spiritual body" (I Cor. 15:42-44). Notice that these verses refer to the resurrection body of believers as imperishable, immortal, glorious, powerful and spiritual.

Those who have part in the "First Resurrection" will have bodies "like" the resurrection body of Jesus. "And just as we have borne the likeness of the earthly man, so shall we bear the likeness of the man from heaven" (I Cor. 15:49). Already in this chapter I cited Phil. 3:20 & 21 which concludes, "...our lowly bodies...will be like his glorious body."

Jesus compared the resurrection body to the angels: "At the resurrection people will neither marry not be given in marriage; they will be like the angels in heaven" (Matt. 22:30).

In the I Thess. 4 passage quoted in the previous section of this chapter, you read, "We...will be caught up together with them in the clouds" (v.17). Greater than we can imagine, will be the blessing of dwelling forever with all the saints of the ages and *being reunited with loved ones* who preceded us to Heaven. I look forward to seeing my parents and other relatives and friends who are with the Lord.

The greatest blessing of the resurrection will be our *living forever in the presence of the Lord Jesus.* "With the same spirit of faith we also believe and therefore speak, because we know that the one who raised the Lord Jesus from the dead will also raise us with Jesus and present us with you in his presence" (II Cor. 4:13, 14). Read again the glorious words of I Thess. 4:17, "And so we will be with the Lord forever."

I conclude this chapter with the prayer in Rev. 22:20, "Amen. Come, Lord Jesus."

CHAPTER 10

REWARDS

*I press on toward the goal to win the prize
for which God has called me heavenward in
Christ Jesus. (Phil. 4:4).*

"All spiritual blessings" include a lot more
than "pie in the sky by and by." Even
though believers have been criticized for looking
forward to rewards in Heaven, it is natural for the
child of God to look forward to eternity with his
heavenly Father. Heaven is not a reward for the righteous; it is a gift for the guilty. However, believers
can look forward to eternal rewards. In this final
chapter we will examine what the Bible says about
those rewards.

THE BLESSINGS OF HEAVENLY REWARDS

Believers look forward to Heaven because of *the*

Christ presenting the rewards. Jesus promised, "Behold, I am coming soon! My reward is with me, and I will give to everyone according to what he has done" (Rev. 22:12). So Jesus will present rewards at the time of His Second Coming. He made a similar promise during His public ministry on earth: "For the Son of Man is going to come in his Father's glory with his angels, and then he will reward each person according to what he has done" (Matt. 16:27).

Rewards will be presented at the Judgment Seat of Christ: "For we must all appear before the judgment seat of Christ, that everyone may receive what is due him for the things done in the body, whether good or bad" (II Cor. 5:10). Believers can look forward to that time if they have heeded the advice of Jesus to "...store up for yourselves treasures in heaven" (Matt. 6:20a). Later in the chapter we will consider how that is done.

Believers will experience the blessing of having Jesus fulfill His promise, "whoever acknowledges me before men, I will acknowledge him before my Father in heaven" (Matt. 10:32). What a blessing it will be to be among those of whom Jesus was thinking when He gave the parable of the Talents and spoke of the master saying to the faithful steward, "Well done, good and faithful servant!" (Matt. 25:21a). May Jesus be able to say that to you and me!

The blessings of Heaven will belong only to those whose *citizenship* is *in Heaven*. Paul wrote to the believers in Ephesus: "...you...are fellow citizens with God's people and members of God's household" (Eph. 2:19). "Therefore, since we are receiving a kingdom that cannot be shaken, let us be thankful, and so worship God acceptably with reverence and awe" (Heb. 12:28). Citizens of Heaven can look forward to rich rewards: "Therefore, my brothers, be all the more eager to make your calling and election sure. For if you do these things, you will never fall, and you will receive a rich welcome into the eternal kingdom of our Lord and Savior Jesus Christ" (II Peter 1:10, 11).

Believers can rejoice in *the certainty of rewards.* "For God is not unrighteous to forget your work and labor of love, which ye have showed toward his name, in that ye have ministered to the saints, and do minister" (Heb. 6:10 KJV). Jesus promised, "And if anyone gives even a cup of cold water to one of these little ones because he is a disciple, I tell you the truth, he will certainly not lose his reward" (Matt. 10:42).

The Bible speaks of several *crowns to be awarded.* The Crown of Life is mentioned twice. In James 1:12 it is said to be awarded to those who have demonstrated their love for God by persevering through trials: "Blessed is the man who perseveres under trial, because when he has stood the test, he will receive the crown of life that God has promised to those who love him." In Rev. 2:10c the Crown of Life is the martyrs crown: "Be faithful, even to the point of death and I will give you the crown of life."

Other crowns include the Crown of Righteousness for those who live in anticipation of our Lord's return: "Now there is in store for me the crown of righteousness which the Lord, the righteous

Judge, will award to me on that day—and not only to me, but also to all who have longed for his appearing" (I Tim. 4:8).The Crown of Glory is promised to faithful pastors: "And when the Chief Shepherd appears, you will receive the crown of glory that will never fade away" (I Peter 5:4). Paul called his reward for founding the church at Thessalonica a Crown of Rejoicing: "For what is our hope, or joy, or crown of rejoicing? Are not ye in the presence of our Lord Jesus Christ at his coming?" (I Thess. 2:19 KJV). The believer who leads a disciplined, Christ-honoring life is promised an Eternal Crown: "Everyone who competes in the games goes into strict training. They do it to get a crown that will not last, but we do it to get a crown that will last forever" (I Cor. 9:25). I desire to win as many crowns as possible so that when I stand before the Throne of God I will have crowns to lay at the feet of Jesus my Lord.

Consider other rewards mentioned in Scripture. One is the promise of rest: "Then I heard a voice from heaven say, 'Write: Blessed are the dead who die in the Lord from now on.' 'Yes,' says the Spirit, 'they will rest from their labor, for their deeds follow them'" (Rev. 14:13). This does not mean that Heaven will be a place of inactivity. Every believer will be involved in activity that will enable him to make enjoyable and satisfying use of his unique talents for all eternity.

Several other rewards are mentioned as Christ's promises to "overcomers" at the conclusion of His message to each of the seven churches mentioned in Revelation chapters 2 and 3. The first of these is:

"To him who overcomes, I will give the right to eat from the tree of life, which is in the paradise of God" (Rev. 2:7b). This reminds us that our rewards will last for all eternity.

The next promise says, "He who overcomes will not be hurt at all by the second death" (Rev. 2:11b). God will erase from our memories everything that would detract from our happiness in Heaven.

Believers are promised heavenly food and a heavenly name: "To him who overcomes, I will give some of the hidden manna. I will also give him a white stone with a new name written on it, known only to him who receives it" (Rev. 2:17b).

In a previous chapter we considered the believer's reward of reigning with Christ. One Scripture reference we did not use in that chapter was Rev. 2:26-28: "To him who overcomes and does my will to the end, I will also give authority over the nations—'He will rule them with an iron scepter; he will dash them to pieces like pottery'—just as I received authority from my Father. I will give him the morning star."

The next promise has to do with the purity of the believer's life in Heaven: "He who overcomes will, like them, be dressed in white. I will never blot out his name from the book of life, but will acknowledge his name before my Father and his angels" (Rev. 3:5).

The sixth promise has to do with the believer's identity in Heaven: "Him who overcomes I will make a pillar in the temple of my God. Never again will he leave it. I will write on him the name of my God and the name of the city of my God, the new

Jerusalem, which is coming down out of heaven from my God; and I will also write on him my new name" (Rev. 3:12)

The final promise to overcomers has to do with honor and position bestowed by Jesus our Lord: "To him who overcomes, I will give the right to sit with me on my throne, just as I overcame and sat down with my Father on his throne" (Rev. 3:21).

THE BASIS OF HEAVENLY REWARDS

What the Bible says about rewards leads to the conclusion that there will be degrees of rewards depending on several factors that God can measure perfectly. One or more of those factors is indicated in the following passage: "For no one can lay any foundation other than the one already laid, which is Jesus Christ. If any man builds on this foundation using gold, silver, costly stones, wood, hay or straw, his work will be shown for what it is, because the Day will bring it to light. It will be revealed with fire, and the fire will test the quality of each man's work. If what he has built survives, he will receive his reward. If it is burned up, he will suffer loss; he himself will be saved, but only as one escaping through the flames" (I Cor. 3:11-15). It is clear that this passage applies only to believers when it speaks of those who are building their lives on Jesus Christ as the only Foundation. The quality of a believer's life is compared to gold, silver, costly stones, wood, hay or straw. God's crucible of testing will refine works of the quality of gold, silver and costly stones, but will burn works of the quality of wood, hay or straw. Then it is important to know what determines *the quality of a believer's works*.

Jesus emphasized the importance of motive in all we do. In His Sermon on the Mount, Jesus warned: "Be careful not to do your 'acts of righteousness' before men, to be seen by them. If you do, you will have no reward from your Father in heaven" (Matt. 6:1). Jesus promised rewards to those who give with *the right motive*: "But when you give to the needy, do not let your left hand know what your right hand is doing, so that your giving may be in secret. Then your Father, who sees what is done in secret, will reward you" (Matt. 6:3, 4). God always knows what you and I do and our motivation for everything we do.

Right motives include *the motive of love*. "But love your enemies, do good to them, and lend to them without expecting to get anything back. Then your reward will be great, and you will be sons of the Most High, because he is kind to the ungrateful and wicked" (Luke 6:35).

Our motivation and the quality of our service will depend in part on our having a *proper reverence for God*. "Since you call on a Father who judges each man's work impartially, live your lives as strangers here in reverent fear" (I Peter 1:17).

In Paul's first letter to the Corinthians he rebuked them for being carnal and not being spiritual believers. That was one reason some of them were performing works only of the quality of wood, hay and straw. They were not *abiding in Christ*, not depending on Him and not being used by Him in their Christian service. Jesus said, "No branch can bear fruit by itself; it must remain in the vine...I am the vine; you are the branches...apart from me you can do nothing" (John 15:4b & 5a&c). When we are living in union with Jesus so that He is working through us, then our works are of the quality of gold, silver and costly stones.

The Bible teaches that every believer has one or more spiritual gifts that should be used in *Christian ministry*. Concerning such ministry we may claim the promise, "The man who plants and the man who waters have one purpose, and each will be rewarded according to his own labor" (I Cor. 3:8).

Believers are promised rewards for *sacrifices made* in following Christ. "You sympathized with those in prison and joyfully accepted the confiscation of your property, because you knew that you yourselves had better and lasting possessions. So do not throw away your confidence; it will be richly rewarded" (Heb. 10:34, 35). Jesus gave the same assurance: "Blessed are you when men hate you, when they exclude you and insult you and reject your name as evil, because of the Son of Man. Rejoice in that day and leap for joy, because great is your reward in heaven" (Luke 6:22, 23a). Jesus also promised, "And everyone who has left houses or brothers or sisters or father or mother or children or fields for my sake will receive a hundred times as much and will inherit eternal life" (Matt. 20:29).

Heavenly rewards will also be determined by *services rendered*. Jesus taught that we serve Him by serving others. In His parable of the King, Jesus said, "The King will reply [to those on his right hand], 'I tell you the truth, whatever you did for one of the least of these brothers of mine, you did for me'" (Matt. 25:40).

The factors mentioned in the above paragraphs would be involved in an evaluation of *good works* that would earn a reward. This may be seen in Paul's instruction to slaves: "Serve wholeheartedly, as if you were serving the Lord, not men, because you know that the Lord will reward everyone for whatever good he does, whether he is slave or free" (Eph. 6:7, 8). This reminds me of the words of Jesus: "But many who are first will be last, and many who are last will be first" (Matt. 19:30). This shows the folly of the attitude expressed on the bumper sticker that says, "The Guy Who Wins Is the One Who Dies with the Most Toys."

Another factor that may be involved in determining rewards is our *having right priorities*. This can be inferred from the following words about Moses: "He regarded disgrace for the sake of Christ as of greater value than the treasures of Egypt, because he was looking ahead to his reward" (Heb. 11:26). Moses took the long look and lived accordingly. God's Word assures us of the wisdom of the choice Moses made. Praise God, the same choice is available to us.

To some extent rewards will be gauged by *quantity* as well as quality. In His parable of the Talents Jesus told of the master who commended the faithful servant for doubling his money. To him the master said, "You have been faithful with a few things; I will put you in charge of many things. Come and share your master's happiness!" (Matt. 25:21b).

The quantity of a believer's service will depend on his *stewardship* of the opportunities, responsibilities and resources with which he has been entrusted. "As each one has received a special gift, employ it in serving one another, as good stewards of the manifold grace of God" (I Peter 4:10 NAS).

In spite of what the Bible reveals about rewards, we cannot adequately appreciate what awaits us in our heavenly home. "'No eye has seen, no ear has heard, no mind has conceived what God has prepared for those who love him'—but God has revealed it to us by his Spirit" (I Cor. 2:9). Thank God that His Word gives us a few glimpses into glory. May we so relate ourselves to our Lord that what was said of Abraham can be said of us: "For he was looking forward to the city with foundations, whose architect and builder is God" (Heb. 11:10).

THE END

Printed in the United States
26370LVS00001B/91-363